POSTCARDS 2

Brian Abbs
Chris Barker
Ingrid Freebairn
with Marcia Fisk Ong
and Stella Reilly

LONGMAN ON THE **WEB**

Longman.com offers online resources for teachers and students. Access our Companion Websites, our online catalog, and our local offices around the world.

Longman English Success offers online courses to give learners flexible study options. Courses cover General English, Business English, and Exam Preparation.

Visit us at **longman.com** and **englishsuccess.com**.

Longman

longman.com

Postcards 2

Pearson Education, 10 Bank Street, White Plains, NY 10606

Vice president, director of publishing: Allen Ascher
Editorial director: Ed Lamprich
Publisher: Sherri Arbogast
Senior development editor: Stella Reilly
Vice president, director of design and production: Rhea Banker
Executive managing editor: Linda Moser
Production manager: Liza Pleva
Associate managing editor: Mike Kemper
Director of manufacturing: Patrice Fraccio
Senior manufacturing buyer: Dave Dickey
Photo research: Aerin Csigay
Cover design: Ann France
Text design: Ann France and Pearson Education Development Group
Text font: 11/14 palatino
Text composition: Pearson Education Development Group

ISBN: 0-13-092585-3

5 6 7 8 9 10–WC–07 06 05

Acknowledgments

The authors and publishers wish to acknowledge with gratitude the following reviewers, contributors, photographers and illustrators who helped in the development of *Postcards 2*:

Reviewers

Celso dos Santos, Brazil • **Claudia Amaya**, Colombia • **Samuel Réales**, Colombia • **María Cristina Merodio Tamés**, Mexico • **JoAnn Miller**, Mexico • **Marc Chevalier**, Peru • **Noela Cartaya de Herrero**, Venezuela

Contributors

Charles Green for writing the games, the projects, and the culture readings. • **David McKeegan** for writing the *"Let's Get Started."* unit.

Illustration credits

pp.2, 3, 11 (top), 17, 19, 22, 35, 40, 47, 53, 56, 69 (border), 78 (col. 2), 82 (top), 83 (top) Mike Hortens; pp.34, 52 Andrew Shiff; pp.13, 41 Anna Veltfort; p.7 Brian Hughes; p.78 Robert Roper; pp.8, 48, 82 (bottom) Tim Haggerty; pp.14, 39, 75 Chris Reed; p.69 Peter Gunther; p.30 Daniel F. Clifford; p.31 Simon Shaw; p.58 Don Dyen; p.59 Alan Neider; pp.77, 91, 92 Ron Zalme; p.87 Jim Starr; p.93 Francois Escalmel

Text credits

p.17 www.chefjustin.com; p.30 "Back Here." Words and music by Christian Burns, Mark Barry, Stephen McNally and Phil Thornalley ©1999, 2000 Strongsongs Ltd. and BMG Music Publishing Ltd. This arrangement ©2002 Strongsongs Ltd. and BMG Music Publishing Ltd. All rights for Strongsongs Ltd. in the U.S. and Canada controlled and administered by EMI April Music Inc. All rights for BMG Music Publishing Ltd. Administered by BMG Songs, Inc. All rights reserved. International copyright secured. Used by permission; p.58 "Baby, Baby." Words and music by Amy Grant and Keith Thomas ©1991 Age to age Music, Inc. (Admin. by The Loving Company), BMG Songs, Inc. and Yellow Elephant Music, Inc. This arrangement ©2002 Age to age Music, Inc. (Admin. by The Loving Company), BMG Songs, Inc. and Yellow Elephant Music, Inc. All rights Reserved. Used by permission; p.64 Solo Syndication for adapted extracts from the article "Lightning blasts tent teenagers" by Angela Mollard in the Daily Mail; p.78 Adapted from The Book of You. © by Sylvia Funston. HarperCollins Publishers, Inc. All rights reserved; p.86 "The One." Words and music by Max Martin and Brian T. Littrell ©1999 Zomba Enterprises Inc./B-ROK Publishing/Zomba Music Publishers Ltd. All rights on behalf of B-ROK Publishing administered by Zomba Enterprises Inc. for the World and all rights on behalf of Zomba Music Publishers Ltd. administered by Zomba Enterprises Inc. for the U.S.A. and Canada. Lyrics reprint by permission of Warner Bros. Publications, Miami, FL 33014. All rights reserved.

Photo credits

All original photography by Stephen Ogilvey; food shots, pp.12 and 20 by Brian and Amy Hutchings; p.3 (1) FPG International/Getty Images, (2) Georgina Bowater/Corbis Stock Market, (3) Michael Newman/PhotoEdit, (4) Jonathan Nourok/PhotoEdit, (5) Rob Lewine/Corbis Stock Market, (6) Jose Galvez/PhotoEdit; p.5 (left) Michael Newman/ PhotoEdit, (right) Tony Freeman/PhotoEdit; p.16 Courtesy Jimi Miller. Photography by Ken Nolfi; p.17 Courtesy Jimi Miller; p.22 Myrleen F. Cate/ PhotoEdit; p.26 (left) Richard Hamilton Smith/ CORBIS, (center) Duomo/CORBIS, (right) Myrleen Ferguson Cate/PhotoEdit, (top) Scott Markewitz/ Getty Images; p.27 (top) David Young-Wolff/PhotoEdit, (center) Kelly-Mooney Photography/CORBIS, (bottom left) Bill Hickey/ Getty Images, (bottom right) Bob Mitchell/ CORBIS; p.28 Scott S. Warren Photography; p.30 PACHA/ Corbis; p.36 (center) Roger Mastroianni/Black Star, (top and bottom) Courtesy of George Vlosich III; p.42 (top) Neal Preston/CORBIS, (center and bottom) Reuters NewMedia Inc./CORBIS; p.44 (left) PhotoDisc/Getty Images, (top) David Young-Wolff/PhotoEdit, (bottom) Paul A. Souders/ Corbis; p.45 Duomo/Corbis; p.50 (1950s) Photofest, (1960s) AKG London, (1970s and 1980s) Bettmann/CORBIS, (1990s) Richard Lord /The Image Works; p.58 Neal Preston/ Corbis; p.60 (top right) Randy Faris/CORBIS, (top left) Sandy Felsenthal/ CORBIS, (center right) Bob Krist/CORBIS, (bottom left and right) Stone/Getty Images, (bottom center) AFP/CORBIS; p.64 Kent News and Pictures Ltd.; p.68 (Women left) Andrew Errington/ Getty Images, (Women center) Donna Day/CORBIS, (Women right) Masterfile, (Sports left) Index Stock Imagery/Eric Sanford, (Sports right) CORBIS, (Sports center) Index Stock Imagery/Murry Sill, (Actors top and bottom) The Everett Collection, (Actors center) Photofest; p.70 (1) The Colossus of Rhodes 3 (detail) by Georg Balthasar Probst, 18th century. Stapleton Collection, UK/ Bridgeman Art Library, (2, 4, 5) Bettmann/ CORBIS, (3) Larry Lee/ CORBIS, (6) Historical Picture Archive/CORBIS, (7) St. Paul Preaching Before the Temple of Diana at Ephesusby Adolf Pirsch, 1885. Phillips, The International Fine Art Auctioneers, UK/ Bridgeman Art Library; p.72 (top) Archivo Iconografico, S.A./ Corbis, (bottom) Mitchell Gerber/ Corbis; p 73 (top right) Danny Lehman/Corbis, (bottom left) AFP/Corbis, (bottom right) Christophe Loviny/Corbis; p.74 Images; p.82 Dallas & John Heaton/CORBIS; p.84 (top right) Myrleen Ferguson Cate/ PhotoEdit, (bottom right) Mary Kate Denny/ PhotoEdit, (left) © Syracuse Newspapers/David Lassman/The Image Works; p.86 Mitchell Gerber/Corbis; p.94 (top right) Jeff Hunter/Getty Images, (left) Bob Krist/CORBIS, (bottom right) Guido Alberto Rossi/Getty Images, (center) Stepehn Frink/CORBIS; p.95 (left) Robert Brenner/ PhotoEdit, (center left) Vic Bider/PhotoEdit, (center right) Elena Rooraid/PhotoEdit, (bottom left) FoodPix/Getty Images, (bottom right) Amet Jean Pierre/Corbis Sygma; pp.96-97 (1) The Image Bank/Getty Images, (2) Chris Rainier/Corbis, (3) Wolfgang Kaehler/CORBIS, (4) Greg Martin/SuperStock, (center) The Image Bank/Getty Images; p.98 (top) Dave Bartruff/CORBIS, (1) Sergio Dorantes/ CORBIS, (2) Margaret Courtney-Clarke/ CORBIS, (3) Ken Goff/TimePix, (4) A. Ramey/PhotoEdit; p.99 Dave Bartruff/ CORBIS; p.100 (top) Paul A. Souders/CORBIS, (1) Lindsay Hebberd/Corbis, (2) Patrick Ward/CORBIS; p.101 (3) Bob Krist/ CORBIS; p.100-101 (4) Paul A. Souders/CORBIS
Cover photos: spotlight © Silver Burdett Ginn; Broadway shows © wonderfile; Kids © John Henley/corbisstockmarket.com; NYC © corbisstockmarket.com; skateboarder © corbisstockmarket.com.

Contents

Scope and Sequence

Vocabulary	Skills	Learn to Learn	Pronunciation
Describing people	*Reading:* Read for specific details; make inferences *Listening:* Listen for specific details to fill in a chart *Speaking:* Describe people *Writing:* Write a descriptive paragraph		
Common cooking ingredients Sequence words: *first, next, then, after that, finally*	*Reading:* Read for specific details *Speaking:* Talk about after-school activities *Listening:* Listen for specific information	Using the dictionary	The sounds /θ/ and /ð/
Food items in the supermarket	*Reading:* Read for specific details *Listening:* Listen to evaluate information *Speaking:* Discuss health habits *Writing:* Write a letter asking for advice	Organizing vocabulary	The sounds /tʃ/ and /ʃ/
Sports	*Reading:* Read for specific details; make inferences *Listening:* Listen for specific details *Speaking:* Talk about abilities; express opinions *Writing:* Write paragraphs		The /ŋ/ sound
Leisure activities	*Reading:* Guess meaning from context *Listening:* Listen for specific information *Writing:* Write a journal entry	Learning how to spell some words	
Clothes	*Reading:* Read for details; make inferences *Listening:* Listen for specific information *Speaking:* Comment on clothes		The sound of *be going to* + verb

Unit	Title	Communication	Grammar

7
 	
Pages 46–51
	You were awesome, Alex!	• Talk about past events
		• Agree or disagree with someone
			• Simple past: regular verbs
			  – Affirmative and negative statements
			  – *Yes/No* questions
			  – Information questions

8 Pages 52–56	**Did you hear the news?**	• Talk about past events • Express opinions	• Simple past: irregular verbs • Coordinate conjunctions: *and*, *but*, *so*
Page 57	Progress Check		

| Page 58 | **Song 2:** Baby, Baby | | |
| Page 59 | **Game 2:** Q and A Baseball | | |

Unit	Title	Communication	Grammar
9 Pages 60–65	**Why didn't you call us?**	• Narrate a past event • Talk about the weather	• The past continuous with *when* and *while* • Simple past contrasted with past continuous
10 Pages 66–70	**Is he better than I am?**	• Ask and express preferences or choices *(Which)*	• Comparative and superlative forms of adjectives • *As* + adjective + *as*
Page 71	Progress Check		

| Pages 72–73 | **Wide Angle 3:** What Is Beauty? | | |

Unit	Title	Communication	Grammar
11 Pages 74–79	**You should get some rest.**	• Give advice	• *Should/Shouldn't* • Habitual past: *used to*

12
 	
Pages 80–84
	Will you call us?	• Express possibility with *may* and *might*	• Simple future: *will*
			  – Affirmative and negative statements
			  – *Yes/No* questions
			• *May* and *might*

Page 85	Progress Check		

| Page 86 | **Song 3:** The One | | |
| Page 87 | **Game 3:** Say and Do the Opposite | | |

Vocabulary	Skills	Learn to Learn	Pronunciation
Past-time markers More clothes	*Reading:* Read a pictorial timeline *Listening:* Listen for specific information *Speaking:* Interview a classmate	Learning meanings of new words through pictures	Stress patterns in past-time markers
Adjectives to describe states of being and feelings	*Reading:* Read for details; draw conclusions *Listening:* Listen for specific information *Speaking:* Express personal opinions *Writing:* Write paragraphs		
Adjectives describing the weather	*Reading:* Identify sentences to support an opinion *Listening:* Listen for specific information to fill in a chart *Speaking:* Express personal opinions *Writing:* Write a narrative about a past experience		
Adjectives	*Reading:* Read for specific details *Speaking:* Express personal opinions; express preferences *Writing:* Write a report based on simple research	Exploring the Internet	Questions with *Which*
Parts of the body Common illnesses	*Reading:* Guess meaning from pictorial representation *Listening:* Listen for specific information *Speaking:* Give advice *Writing:* Write a paragraph about what used to be		
Summer activities	*Reading:* Read for specific information *Speaking:* Talk about future plans *Writing:* Write paragraphs about future plans; do research		The sound /l/ in contractions

Joe   Diane   Alex

Lori   Karen   Paul

Let's get started.

1 Months and Ordinal Numbers

Match the months with the ordinals.

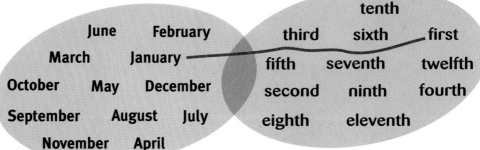

June   February

March   January

October   May   December

September   August   July

November   April

tenth

third   sixth   first

fifth   seventh   twelfth

second   ninth   fourth

eighth   eleventh

2 Seasons

In the United States, what months fall in each season? Write them in the correct column below.

Spring	Summer	Fall	Winter
April			

3 Family

A. Read the clues below. Write the letters in the numbered boxes. What is the mystery word?

1. The first letter of the second month

1	2	3	4	5	6
F					

2. The second letter of the fifth month
3. The fifth letter of the eleventh month
4. The fourth letter of the fourth month
5. The third letter of the seventh month
6. The seventh letter of the first month.

B. Do the family crossword puzzle. Use the words in the box.

cousin   father   mother   brother   sister
uncle   aunt   son   daughter   parents

Across

1. My father's brother is my _____.
4. I am her mother. She is my _____.
6. I am his father. He is my _____.
7. My father's sister is my _____.
8. My "mom" is my _____.
9. This boy's mother and father are my mother and father, too. This boy is my _____.

Down

2. Her father is my uncle. She is my _____.
3. My mother and father are my _____.
5. My "dad" is my _____.
6. This girl's mother and father are my mother and father, too. This girl is my _____.

4 Occupations

A. Look at the pictures. Fill in the blanks with one of the occupations in the box below.

musicians	engineer	accountant
teacher	firefighter	politician

1. My father is a _____firefighter_____.

2. My mother is an _____.

3. My cousin is an _____.

4. My aunt is a _____.

5. My sister is a _____.

6. My brothers are _____.

B. Work with a partner. Play *What's My Job*? Student A chooses an occupation. Student B asks *Yes/No* questions to try to guess what it is. Student B can ask a maximum of ten questions.

B: Do you use a computer?
A: Yes, I do.
B: Are you an accountant?
A: No, I'm not.
B: Do you work in an office?

Let's get started. *3*

Crossword puzzle

¹U N ²C L E

We're members of Teen Scenes.

Learning Goals

Communication
Ask for and give personal information
Ask for and give physical descriptions

Grammar
Simple present of *be*: review
Possessive pronouns: *mine, yours, his, hers, ours, theirs*

Vocabulary
Describing people

1 Reading

🎧 **Listen and read. Circle the names of Lori's best friends.**

Hi. My name's Alex Romero, and I'm 15 years old. I'm an actor and a musician. I play the guitar. I'm a member of Teen Scenes, a drama and music group.

Hi. I'm Joe Sanders. I'm also 15. I like reading, music, and basketball. I hang out with Alex all the time. He's my best friend.

Hello. I'm Diane Sanders. I'm Joe's sister. I'm 14. I'm also in Teen Scenes.

I'm Paul Chan, the director of Teen Scenes. I'm 30 years old. I love the theater.

Hey. I'm Lori Hudson. I'm 15. Diane and Karen are my best friends. I'm in Teen Scenes, too. I love it!

My name is Karen Jackson, and I'm 14 years old. I'm from California. Now I live in New York City, and I love it! I'm part of Teen Scenes. I want to be in a Broadway show one day.

GRAMMAR FOCUS

Review of be

Yes/No questions

Am	I	
Are	you	
Is	he/she/it	good?
Are	we/they	

Affirmative answers

Yes, you **are**.
Yes, I **am**.
Yes, he/she/it **is**.
Yes, we/they **are**.

Negative answers

No, you **aren't**.
No, I'**m not**.
No, he/she/it **isn't**.
No, we/they **aren't**.

Remember! Contractions: subject pronoun + be

I am	= **I'm**	she is	= **she's**	he is	= **he's**
you are	= **you're**	we are	= **we're**	they are	= **they're**

2 Practice

A. Fill in the blanks with the correct form of the verb be. You may use contractions. Then look at the two photographs. Label Francis.

_____   _____

Hello! My name (1) __'s__ Francis. I (2) ____ from Connecticut. I (3) ____ 15 years old, and I (4) ____ a high-school student. I have brown eyes and straight, black hair. I (5) ____ a football player at my high school. I love sports!

I have one sister. Her name (6) ____ Angela. She (7) ____ 13. Angela has a birthday only once every four years! Why? Because her birthday is on February 29th. Angela (8) ____ on the girls' soccer team at her school. She says she (9) ____ a better soccer player than I am, but she (10) ____ (negative)!

B. Work with a partner. Ask and answer Yes/No questions about the information in the paragraphs above.

A: Is Francis a baseball player?
B: No, he's not. He's a football player.

3 Practice

Have a competition! Turn to page 88.

GRAMMAR FOCUS

Information questions with be

Questions	Long answers
Who **is** she?	She'**s** my teacher.
What **is** her name?	Her name'**s** Sandra Perkins.
How old **is** she?	She'**s** 28 years old.
Where **are** they from?	They'**re** from Canada.
When **is** your next class?	It'**s** tomorrow.

Remember!

Who is = **Who's**
What is = **What's**
When is = **When's**

4 Practice

Write five information questions about the paragraphs in Exercise 2A. Use who, what, how old, where, and when.

1. _Who's from Connecticut?_
2. _____
3. _____
4. _____
5. _____
6. _____

5 Dialogue

🎧 **Listen and read.**

Mom: Good morning, kids.

Diane: Morning, Mom. Hey Joe, that's my magazine!

Joe: No, it's not. It's mine!

Diane: Yeah, right. You know it's mine, Joe.

Joe: OK, OK. It's yours, but can I look at it?

Diane: Hmm. Let me guess. You want to check out Jessica Simpson, right? Or Destiny's Child?

Joe: Destiny's Child, of course. They're beautiful! They're tall and thin . . . and they can move!

Diane: Keep dreaming, Joe.

Dad: OK. That's enough, you two. So, how's Teen Scenes, Diane?

Diane: Fine, Dad, but we need a lot of practice. Our show is in four weeks!

Joe: Too bad it isn't in forty weeks —you need it!

Mom: Joe, was that necessary?

6 Comprehension

Read the sentences. Write *T* for true and *F* for false.

_F_ 1. The magazine is Joe's.

____ 2. Joe likes Destiny's Child.

____ 3. The women in Destiny's Child are tall.

____ 4. The members of Teen Scenes need to practice.

____ 5. The Teen Scenes' show is in forty weeks.

GRAMMAR FOCUS

Possessive pronouns

Subject	Possessive	
I	**mine**	This book is **mine**.
You	**yours**	That book is **yours**.
She	**hers**	This book is **hers**.
He	**his**	Those books are **his**.
We	**ours**	These books are **ours**.
They	**theirs**	That book is **theirs**.

Question with *whose*	Answer
Whose book is that?	It's mine.

7 Practice

Fill in the blanks with possessive pronouns. Use the subject pronoun in parentheses as your cue.

1. Those CDs are ___*theirs*___ (*they*).

2. That backpack is _____ (*she*).

3. The soccer ball is _____ (*we*).

4. Please don't take that comic book.
   It's_____ (*I*).

5. Those sneakers aren't mine. They're
   _____ (*he*).

6. This isn't my cell phone. It's _____ (*you*).

8 Practice

Work with a partner. Write questions and answers about the sentences in Exercise 7. Use *Whose* in your questions.

1. Q: _*Whose CDs are those?*_

   A: _*They're theirs.*_

2. Q: _____

   A: _____

3. Q: _____

   A: _____

4. Q: _____

   A: _____

5. Q: _____

   A: _____

6. Q: _____

   A: _____

9 Listening

🎧 **Listen to the conversation. Put a check under the name of the person who owns each object.**

Object	Isabel	Lukas	Michael
CDs/CD player			✔
Walkman			
video game			
magazines			
basketball			

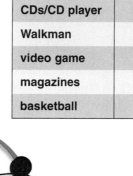

10 Vocabulary

Describing people

A. Match the descriptions with the pictures below. Write the names in the blanks.

Sid 1. He's tall and thin. He has straight, black hair. He's nice, but he's usually serious.

_____ 2. She's a bit heavy. Her height is average. She has curly, blond hair. She's pretty and very friendly.

_____ 3. She's short. She has wavy, red hair. She's not heavy. She's not thin either. She's smart, but she's shy.

_____ 4. He's tall and strong. He has brown hair. He's really funny.

B. Work with a partner. Underline the physical descriptions in Exercise A. Circle the personality traits.

11 Practice

Work with a partner. Take turns describing and guessing the names of the characters on page 4.

A: He's handsome. He has a medium build. His hair is straight and black. He loves the theater.

B: Is it Paul?

12 Your Turn

Work in groups of five. Write a description of yourself. Don't write your name! Swap paragraphs. Read the paragraph you receive out loud. Your group members will guess who that person is.

I'm 14. My height is average. My hair's brown and wavy. I have brown eyes. I'm very shy.

The New Director

Read the story and write the missing sentences. Choose from the box on the right. Then listen and check your work.

He's tall and thin.
What does he look like?
Who can we ask?
What's his name?
He's a good guitar player.

1. Hi, Diane. / Hey, Karen. What's up?

2. Nothing much. / Guess what? We have a new director for Teen Scenes! / (1) _____ / Paul.

3. (2) _____ Is he handsome? / Very. (3) _____ He's nice too.

4. Cool. Hey, don't forget, we still need a guitar player. (4) _____ / Maybe we can ask Alex. (5) _____

5. Alex, of course. The man of your dreams... / Oh, don't be silly.

6. By the way, I need to practice our song. Would you like to do it together? / Great idea. Let's do it on Friday.

Unit 1   9

2 Let's make pizza.

Communication
Give and follow instructions

Grammar
Count and noncount nouns
There is/There are with *some*
and *any*

Vocabulary
Common cooking ingredients
Sequence words: *first, next, then,
after that, finally*

1 Dialogue

🎧 **Listen and read. Circle the ingredients for
the pizza.**

Joe: I'm so hungry. What can we eat?

Alex: How about pizza? Let's make a
chocolate chip pizza!

Joe: OK. Let's go for it! What do we need?

Alex: To start, we need some pizza dough.

Joe: There's some dough in the fridge.

Alex: Great. First, we flatten the
dough. Then we form it into a
large circle.

Joe: And after that?

Alex: After that, we add some
chocolate chips. Do you have any?

Joe: Sure. We use them a lot—well,
usually for cookies.

Alex: Good. Next, we sprinkle nuts on
top. And finally, we bake it in
the oven for about ten minutes.

Diane: Hey, guys. What in the world
are you making?

Alex: We're making a chocolate
chip pizza!

Diane: Gross!

2 Comprehension

Work with a partner. Write down the five steps for making chocolate chip pizza.

1. *First, flatten the dough.*
2. _____
3. _____
4. _____
5. _____

3 Vocabulary

Sequence words

Put the steps in this recipe in the right order. Then add the appropriate sequence words: *first, next, then, after that,* and *finally*.

Scrambled Eggs

( ) _____ stir the eggs, so they don't burn.

( ) _____ melt 1 teaspoon of butter in a medium-size frying pan.

( ) _____ spoon the eggs onto a plate and eat them!

(1) _First_ crack some eggs into a bowl and beat them.

( ) _____ pour the eggs into the frying pan.

4 Communication

Talking about routines

Work with a partner. Ask and answer questions about what you do after school. Use some of the words below and your own ideas. Use sequence words.

watch TV	do my homework
listen to music	play video games
get together with friends	have a snack
chat on the Internet	talk on the phone
spend time with my family	

A: What do you do after school?
B: Well, first, I have a snack. Then, I usually watch TV.

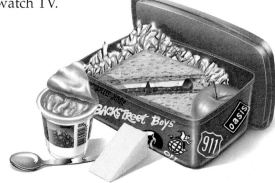

5 Vocabulary

Common cooking ingredients

A. 🎧 Listen and repeat.

__8__ butter	_____ tomato	_____ sugar
_____ potato	_____ rice	_____ milk
_____ water	_____ egg	_____ salt
_____ garlic	_____ oil	_____ cheese
_____ onion	_____ flour	_____ pepper

B. Now match each picture with the correct word in Exercise A. Write the number next to each word.

Count and noncount nouns

Count nouns can be counted.

Singular	Plural
an egg	eggs
a tomato	tomatoes

Noncount nouns *cannot* be counted.

flour   salt   water   sugar

Remember! Use *an* before a singular count noun that begins with a vowel; *a* before a singular count noun that begins with a consonant. Do not add *–s* or *–es* to noncount nouns.

6 Practice

Work with a partner. Look at the words in Exercise 5. In your notebook, list them as count or noncount nouns.

GRAMMAR FOCUS

There is/There are with some and any

Affirmative statements

There's   a tomato
There's   **some** butter   } in the refrigerator.
There are   **some** tomatoes

Yes/No questions

Is there   a tomato
Is there   **some/any** butter   } in the refrigerator?
Are there   **some/any** tomatoes

Negative statements

There isn't   a tomato
There isn't   **any** butter   } here.
There aren't   **any** tomatoes

Short answers

Affirmative	Negative
Yes, there is.	No, there isn't.
Yes, there are.	No, there aren't.

Remember! Use *some* in affirmative sentences and *any* in negative ones. Use *some* and *any* in questions.

7 Practice

Fill in the blanks with *some* or *any*.

1. There isn't _____any_____ food in the kitchen.
2. I don't have _____ money right now.
3. There are _____ apples in the basket.
4. There is _____ juice, too.
5. No, thank you. I don't want _____ juice.
6. Is there _____ milk in the refrigerator?
7. Are there _____ snacks on the table?
8. There aren't _____ cookies in the pantry.
9. There are _____ bananas for you.

9 Pronunciation

The sounds of *th*

A. ⌒ Listen and repeat.

/θ/	/ð/
three	there
thin	them
thought	those

B. ⌒ Listen and circle the word you hear.

1. three   tree
2. tin   thin
3. those   toes
4. tanks   thanks

8 Practice

Work with a partner. Ask and answer questions about the food items in the boxes.

A: Are there any potatoes in the box?
B: No, there aren't. Is there any sugar in the box?
A: Yes, there is.

10 Reading

Before you read, answer these questions in class.

1. Where do you think pizza is originally from?
2. What are your favorite pizza toppings?

Now read the story.

Pizza: The Real Story!

Can you believe that there are just three simple ingredients for one of the world's best-loved snacks? Well, it's true. All you need to make pizza dough is some flour, water, and yeast.

The word *pizza* was used long ago in the year 997 in Italy. At that time pizza looked very different. At first, Romans cooked dough on hot stones. They shaped the dough into disks, and put some onions, garlic, olive oil, and vinegar on them. In the eighteenth century tomatoes were added to pizzas. Now we usually think of pizza as baked dough with tomato sauce and cheese, but there are many different toppings. Pepperoni, olives, onions, and even pineapple are some of the toppings on pizza now.

Today pizza can be found all over the world. It is a very popular food for both children and adults. Whenever parents ask their children what they want for dinner, you can hear them answer, "Pizza, please!"

11 Comprehension

Answer the questions orally.

1. What are the three ingredients in pizza dough?
2. What were the original pizza toppings?
3. What are pizzas topped with today?

12 Listening

🎧 **Listen twice to the report. Then circle the correct answer.**

1. This report is about ____.
   a. the history of chocolate
   b. chocolate recipes from around the world

2. Chocolate comes from the ____ of the cacao tree.
   a. root   b. beans

3. The Olmecs probably made the first chocolate ____.
   a. candy   b. drink

4. The word *chocolate* comes from the word ____.
   a. cacao   b. xocolatl

5. A famous ____ explorer brought chocolate to Europe in the sixteenth century.
   a. Spanish b. French

Learn to Learn

Using the dictionary

The dictionary is an excellent tool to help you learn words in English. Look up the following words in your dictionary:

chop   stir
wash   bake

Progress Check *Units 1 and 2*

A. Change the underlined words to possessive pronouns. Then rewrite the sentences using possessive pronouns. (2 points each)

1. A: Is this your baseball cap?
    B: No, it's not <u>my baseball cap</u>. It's <u>his baseball cap</u>. <u>My baseball cap</u> says "Yankees" on it.

    No, it's not mine. It's his. Mine says "Yankees"

    on it.

2. A: Are these your CDs?
    B: No, they're <u>his CDs</u>. <u>My CDs</u> are in my backpack.

    _____

    A: Can I borrow <u>your CDs</u>?

    _____

3. A: Is this their car?
    B: No. <u>Their car</u> is parked over there.

    _____

    A: So, whose car is this?
    B: It's <u>our car</u>.

    _____

B. Is the underlined noun count or noncount? Write *C* or *NC* next to each sentence. (1 point each)

__NC__ 1. I need some <u>water</u>.

_____ 2. His <u>books</u> are in the backpack.

_____ 3. Mom drinks <u>coffee</u> every morning.

_____ 4. You can have only three <u>cookies</u>.

_____ 5. We get <u>homework</u> every day.

_____ 6. Let's order <u>pizza</u>!

_____ 7. I like <u>lemonade</u>.

_____ 8. Study these <u>words</u>.

C. Write sentences using *there is/there are* with *some* and *any*. Use the cues below. (2 points each)

1. butter / on the table

    There is some butter on the table.

2. orange juice (not) / in the glass

    _____

3. eggs / in the box

    _____

4. milk / in the refrigerator

    _____

5. cookies (not) / in the jar

    _____

6. money (not) / in my wallet

    _____

D. Cross out the adjective that does not belong in each row. (1 point each)

1. funny	~~gray~~	serious
2. thin	heavy	friendly
3. wavy	curly	funny
4. short	long	red
5. shy	handsome	athletic
6. tall	short	smart

E. Number the directions for using a soda machine in the correct sequence. Then write the appropriate sequence words. (2 points each)

__ _____ press the correct button.

__ _____ wait for the soda.

_1_ _First,_ decide what you want.

__ _____ remove the soda and enjoy it!

__ _____ insert your money in the machine.

1 Reading

Scan or read the article on Justin quickly and look for the answers to the following:

_____11_____	1. Justin's age
_____	2. The hotel chain Justin was consultant for
_____	3. The cooking school Justin goes to
_____	4. Justin's former job at Heinz
_____	5. The cookbook Justin wrote

2 Listening

🎧 **Listen to the recipe and instructions for making the Heinz Ketchup Ice Cream Float. Then listen again and complete the recipe card.**

Heinz Ketchup Ice Cream Float

(a) ____2____ tablespoons raspberry jam   Ginger ale

(b) _____ tablespoon Heinz Ketchup   Chocolate sauce

(c) _____ scoops (d) _____ ice cream

First, blend the jam and the (e) _____. Set this mixture aside. Next, fill a tall glass two-thirds full with ginger ale. Then, add the (f) _____ and top it with a spoonful of the Heinz ketchup-raspberry mixture. Finally, drizzle with some (g) _____ sauce.

3 Speaking

Work with a partner. Check each other's recipe cards by asking questions.

A: How many tablespoons of raspberry jam are there in the recipe?

B: Two tablespoons. How about ginger ale? How much do we need?

A: Two-thirds of a glass.

4 Writing

Do this as group homework. Go to *http://www.chefjustin.com* **on the Internet or find a cookbook for kids. Choose a simple recipe. Write the ingredients and the instructions on an index card. In class, swap recipes with other groups.**

Cooking with Chef Justin

Imagine this: You're not even twelve years old, and a major hotel chain and a famous ketchup company offer you a job. Would you accept? Eleven-year-old Justin Miller did. He was a menu consultant for the Marriott Hotels and a former spokesperson for Heinz Ketchup. He is also the author of a kid's cookbook titled *Cooking with Justin*.

Why did the Marriott hotels need Justin's advice? Most kid's menus are the same in every restaurant. "You see chicken fingers every place you go," Justin says. Marriott wanted more variety, so they asked Justin for some help.

At 11, Justin Miller is the world's youngest chef, according to the *Guinness Book of World Records 2002*. The fifth grader has been on TV more than 200 times and goes to cooking school at Johnson and Wales University in Providence, Rhode Island. He first appeared on the *David Letterman Show* at the age of five. These days, Justin is busy with TV appearances, newspaper and magazine interviews, and travel.

Would you like to try one of Justin's recipes for kids like you? Try making Heinz Ketchup Ice Cream Float with your parents.

3 How much do we need?

Learning Goals

Communication
Ask and answer questions about quantity

Grammar
Questions with *How much?/How many?*
Expressions of quantity: *a little, a few, a lot of*

Vocabulary
Common food items in the supermarket

1 Dialogue

🎧 **Scan the dialogue. Circle two examples of junk food. Then listen and read.**

Mom: Hi, Alex. Are you busy today, kids?

Alex: Hi, Mrs. Sanders. No, we're just hanging out.

Mom: Great. Joe can run to the supermarket for me then.

Joe: Me? Go to the supermarket? Come on, Mom. Ask Diane!

Alex: It's OK, Joe. I'll go with you.

Mom: Thanks, Alex. I need bread, milk, eggs, juice, cheese, and ham . . .

Joe: Whoa, Mom. Let me write those down. How much of each do we need?

Mom: Let's start from the top. One loaf of bread, a gallon of milk, a dozen eggs, a half gallon of orange juice, and a half pound each of cheese and ham.

Joe: Mom, slow down! OK. What else?

Mom: One roasting chicken, one bag of onions, six tomatoes, a head of lettuce, and a bunch of carrots.

Joe: Let me repeat what you just said: chicken, onions, tomatoes, lettuce, carrots, chips, and ice cream.

Mom: Good try, Joe. I think we have enough junk food in the house!

Equivalents:
1 pound = about 1/2 kilogram
1 quart = about 1 liter
1 gallon = about 4 liters

2 Comprehension

This is Joe's list. Read the dialogue again and correct Joe's mistakes.

1 loaf of bread
one ~~half~~ gallon of milk
1 dozen eggs
1 gallon of orange juice
1 pound of cheese
1 pound of ham
1 roasting chicken
2 bags of onions
9 tomatoes
2 heads of lettuce
1 bunch of carrots

GRAMMAR FOCUS

Questions with *How much* and *How many*

Questions	Answers
How many bananas do you eat each week?	One or two.
How much juice do you drink each day?	Two glasses.

Remember! Use *how many* with count nouns and *how much* with noncount nouns.

3 Practice

Fill in the blanks in the questionnaire with *How much* or *How many*. Then ask a partner the questions. Circle your partner's answers.

How Healthy Are You?

According to Teenfit.com, a website on teen health, teenagers in the United States don't eat right. Do you eat right? Take this quiz and see.

1. _____ water do you drink each day?
   a. four glasses or more
   b. two glasses
   c. one glass or less

2. _____ servings of vegetables do you eat each day?
   a. two or more
   b. one
   c. none

3. _____ candy and chocolate do you eat each day?
   a. a lot
   b. a little
   c. none

4. _____ pieces of fruit do you eat each day?
   a. two or more
   b. one
   c. none

5. _____ soda do you drink each day?
   a. three glasses or more
   b. one to two glasses
   c. none

4 Vocabulary

Food and drink

🎧 **Match the words and the pictures. Write the numbers. Then listen and check your answers.**

_14_ bread   _____ orange juice

_____ milk   _____ ham

_____ lettuce   _____ strawberries

_____ bananas   _____ grapes

_____ chicken   _____ cookies

_____ carrots   _____ fish

_____ pasta   _____ yogurt

_____ beans   _____ cereal

5 Practice

Work with a partner. First, look up the meanings of the headings below. Then list some foods under the correct headings.

Vegetables	Fruit	Dairy	Grains	Meat
carrots				

6 Pronunciation

The sounds /tʃ/ and /ʃ/

A. 🎧 Listen and repeat.

/tʃ/	/ʃ/
cheese	**sh**eep
chicken	**Sh**elly
chop	**sh**op
pit**ch**	fi**sh**

B. 🎧 Listen and repeat the sentences. Write *ch* or *sh* in the blank.

_____ 1. I'll chop the chicken and the cheese.

_____ 2. Shelly always shops with Sherry.

_____ 3. I like chicken with cheese stuffing.

7 Communication

Asking questions about quantity

A. 🎧 Listen and read.

A: How much bread do we need?

B: Just one loaf. And how many eggs do we need?

A: A dozen.

B. Work with a partner. Pretend you are Joe and Alex at the supermarket. Ask each other how many food items you need to buy. Use the corrected list in Exercise 2.

GRAMMAR FOCUS

Expressions of quantity

Count	Noncount
a few grapes	**a little** milk
a lot of grapes	**a lot of** milk

Remember! Use *a few* with count nouns, and *a little* with noncount nouns. Use *a lot of* with both count and noncount nouns.

8 Practice

Read the dialogue. Underline the correct answer; cross out the wrong one.

Alex: Hey, Joe. I think we're in (1. ~~a few~~, a lot of) trouble. We got a lot of junk food!

Joe: It's not a lot, Alex. It's only (2. a little, a few) bags of chips and (3. a few, a little) boxes of cookies. Of course, (4. a few, a little) ice cream would have been nice, but Mom doesn't want ice cream in the house.

Alex: So how much money is left?

Joe: (5. A few, A little). Of the $100, I have $2.00 left.

Alex: Oh man. I don't think I want to go back home with you.

Joe: You're coming home with me, Alex. We have (6. a little, a lot of) bags to carry.

9 Listening

🎧 **Listen to the conversation. Then write *T* for *true*, *F* for *false*, *NI* for *no information*.**

__T__ 1. Rick exercises a lot.

_____ 2. Rick does a few sit-ups every morning.

_____ 3. Rick has good self-discipline.

_____ 4. Grace doesn't eat a lot of meat.

_____ 5. Grace wants to go to the gym with Rick.

10 Your Turn

In groups, talk about what you eat. Use *a little*, *a few*, *a lot of*, and *some* to describe your diet.

A: What kinds of food do you eat every day?

B: I eat a lot of fruit and vegetables every day.

A: What about junk food? How much junk food do you eat?

11 Reading

Tina writes an Internet column for teens. She gives advice on health. Below is her response to an e-mail from a person who often feels very tired. Read her letter and answer the questions below.

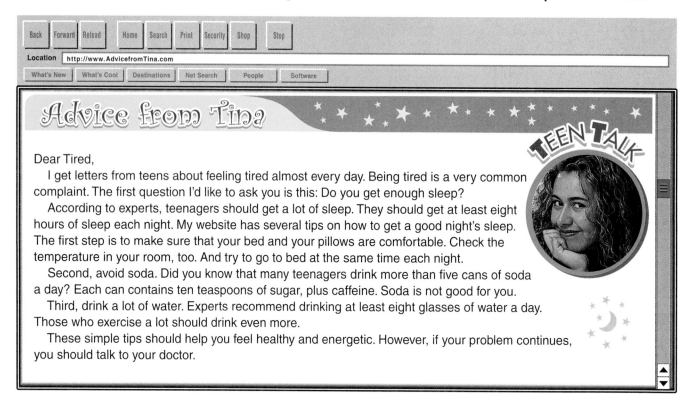

| Back | Forward | Reload | | Home | Search | Print | Security | Shop | | Stop |

Location http://www.AdvicefromTina.com

| What's New | What's Cool | Destinations | Net Search | People | Software |

Advice from Tina ★ ★ ★ ★ ★ ★ ★ ★ ★ ★ ★

TEEN TALK

Dear Tired,

I get letters from teens about feeling tired almost every day. Being tired is a very common complaint. The first question I'd like to ask you is this: Do you get enough sleep?

According to experts, teenagers should get a lot of sleep. They should get at least eight hours of sleep each night. My website has several tips on how to get a good night's sleep. The first step is to make sure that your bed and your pillows are comfortable. Check the temperature in your room, too. And try to go to bed at the same time each night.

Second, avoid soda. Did you know that many teenagers drink more than five cans of soda a day? Each can contains ten teaspoons of sugar, plus caffeine. Soda is not good for you.

Third, drink a lot of water. Experts recommend drinking at least eight glasses of water a day. Those who exercise a lot should drink even more.

These simple tips should help you feel healthy and energetic. However, if your problem continues, you should talk to your doctor.

12 Comprehension

Write the answers in the blanks.

___8___ 1. How many hours of sleep do teenagers need?

_____ 2. How much soda do many teenagers drink?

_____ 3. How many teaspoons of sugar does a can of soda contain?

_____ 4. How much water should we drink every day?

13 Writing

In your notebook, write a letter to Tina. Ask her for advice on any health issues you are interested in.

Dear Tina,
Hi. I'm 13 years old, and I need your help. I hate vegetables, but my mom said they're good for me. I really can't eat them. I think vegetables are yucky. What can I do?

Learn to Learn

Organizing Vocabulary

A good technique to learn new words that belong to a large group is to learn words by category. Look at your list of food items in Exercise 5, page 20. Memorize the items under each category.

Alex and Green Fire

🎧 Read the story and write the missing sentences. Choose from the box on the right. Then listen and check your work.

> Are you asking me to play with Green Fire?
> That's a great name.
> what's the name of your singing group?
> I have a lot of time!
> How can I help?

Hi, Lori. Hi, Karen.

Hi, Alex.

Hey, Lori,
(1) _____

Green Fire.

Green Fire.
(2) _____

Thanks. We like it, too. By the way, Alex, we have a favor to ask you.

Sure. (3) _____

Well, we need a guitar player for our next performance.

(4) _____

Yes, if you have a little extra time.

For you, girls,
(5) _____

Thanks, Alex. We'll get together soon.

4 How often do you skate?

Learning Goals

Communication
Talk about abilities and leisure activities

Grammar
How often . . . ?
Adverbs of frequency
Gerunds

Vocabulary
Sports and leisure activities

1 Dialogue

🎧 **Listen and read. Circle Alex's favorite sport.**

Lori: Hi, Alex. What's up?

Alex: Nothing much. You're pretty good on those skates, Lori.

Lori: Thanks! I love skating.

Alex: How often do you skate?

Lori: Every day. Do you skate too?

Alex: Well, I own a pair of skates. Seriously, you know I'm into basketball.

Lori: Is basketball your only sport?

Alex: Not really. I also go surfing, biking, swimming, skateboarding . . .

Karen: Yeah, yeah, yeah.

Alex: By the way, where's Joe?

Karen: You know Joe's a real couch potato. All he does is read and watch basketball on TV!

Diane: Come on, Karen! He bowls, too.

Karen: Really? How often does he go bowling?

Diane: About three times a year.

2 Comprehension

Circle the correct answer.

1. How often does Lori go skating?
   a. once a week
   b. twice a month
   c. every day

2. What sport does Joe like to watch on TV?
   a. soccer
   b. basketball
   c. baseball

3. A couch potato is a person who _____.
   a. likes to sit and watch TV
   b. likes to eat potato chips
   c. likes vegetables

3 Useful Phrases

A. Write the letter of the correct response to the expressions on the left.

_____ 1. You're pretty good.
_____ 2. What's up?
_____ 3. Is reading your only hobby?

a. Nothing much.
b. Not really. I'm also into sports.
c. Thanks.

B. Practice the expressions and their responses with a partner.

4 Pronunciation

The /ŋ/ sound

A. ⌒ Listen and repeat.

/ŋ/
skating   biking
surfing   swimming

B. ⌒ Listen and repeat. Circle the words with the /ŋ/ sound.

1. Lori likes skating and acting.
2. Alex often goes surfing and swimming.
3. The skating rink is packed today.

5 Vocabulary

Sports

Read the words below and look at the pictures. Write *T* if the sport is a team sport, *I* if it is an individual sport.

_I_ skateboarding __ biking __ soccer

__ running __ baseball __ volleyball

__ in-line skating __ basketball __ gymnastics

__ windsurfing __ swimming __ skiing

GRAMMAR FOCUS

Gerunds as objects of verbs

I like **playing** basketball.	It stopped **working**.
He loves **dancing**.	We enjoyed **windsurfing**.
She hates **running**.	They finished **practicing**.

Remember! These verbs can be followed by gerunds: *like, hate, go, love, enjoy, finish.*

---

6 Practice

Fill in the blanks with the gerund form of the verbs in parentheses.

1. Kate enjoys *(sing)* __singing__.

2. She doesn't like *(dance)* _____.

3. Why did you stop *(practice)* _____?

4. Did you go *(skate)* _____ yesterday?

5. My parents finished *(work)* _____ late last night.

6. They hate *(swim)* _____.

7. Look! It stopped *(rain)* _____.

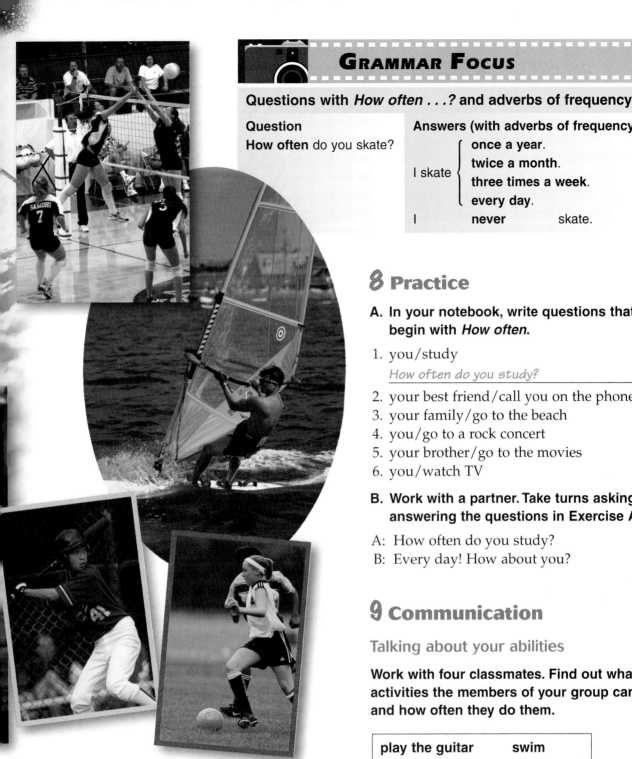

GRAMMAR FOCUS

Questions with *How often . . .?* and adverbs of frequency

Question	Answers (with adverbs of frequency)
How often do you skate?	I skate { once a year. twice a month. three times a week. every day.
	I never skate.

8 Practice

A. In your notebook, write questions that begin with *How often*.

1. you/study

   How often do you study?

2. your best friend/call you on the phone
3. your family/go to the beach
4. you/go to a rock concert
5. your brother/go to the movies
6. you/watch TV

B. Work with a partner. Take turns asking and answering the questions in Exercise A.

A: How often do you study?
B: Every day! How about you?

9 Communication

Talking about your abilities

Work with four classmates. Find out what activities the members of your group can do and how often they do them.

play the guitar	swim
dance the samba	skateboard
ice skate	bike

A: Can you play the guitar?
B: Yes, I can.
A: How often do you play?
B: This year? Never. I'm too busy. How about you?

7 Your Turn

Work with a partner. Ask each other these questions. Use your own information.

1. What do you enjoy doing in your free time?
2. What do your classmates like doing in English class?
3. What do they hate doing in English class?

10 Reading

Read Allison Jones's story.
Underline her philosophy.

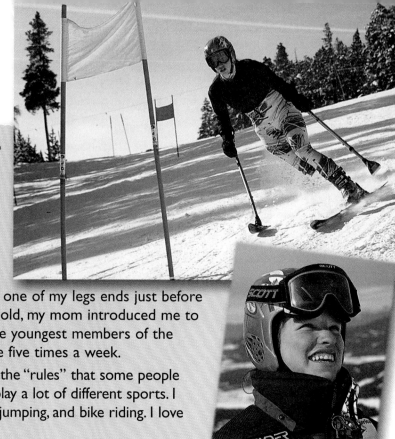

Skiing Isn't My Only Challenge

If there is snow in the mountains, you can find me there. I love flying down ski slopes and competing in downhill races.

By the way, did I mention that I have only one leg? I was born with a defect, so one of my legs ends just before the knee. However, when I was five years old, my mom introduced me to skiing. Now I'm sixteen, and I'm one of the youngest members of the United States Disabled Ski Team. I practice five times a week.

Even though I'm disabled, I don't follow the "rules" that some people think disabled kids should follow. I like to play a lot of different sports. I like rock climbing, swimming, running, high jumping, and bike riding. I love bike riding, so I go every weekend.

You know one thing that really bothers me? People who don't give anything a try. The only way to get ahead in sports—or anything—is to try. My philosophy is simple: If I can do it, I'll do it. If I can't, I'll just try harder.

11 Comprehension

Discuss these questions as a class.

1. What is special about Allison?
2. What are her favorite sports?
3. What bothers her?

12 Listening

🎧 **Listen twice to the radio news. Then fill in the missing information.**

1. Earle Connor is __*Athlete*__ of the Year.

2. He is from _____, Canada.

3. Earle's left leg was amputated when he was _____ years old.

4. Earle holds the record for the 100 meters, the _____ meters, and the long jump.

5. In _____, he was inducted into Calgary's Sports Hall of Fame.

13 Speaking

Work with three classmates. Discuss the following questions:

1. What makes Allison and Earle extraordinary athletes?
2. What lesson can you learn from them?

14 Writing

In your notebook, write about your favorite activity. You can start your paragraph like Allison did.

If there are big waves at the beach, you can find me there. I love surfing . . .

Progress Check *Units 3 and 4*

Grammar

A. Write *How much* or *How many* to complete the questions. (2 points each)

1. _How much_ food do you need?
2. _____ books do you read every week?
3. _____ classmates do you have?
4. _____ money do you need for a CD?
5. _____ milk do you usually drink?

B. Answer the questions with *a little* or *a few*. (2 points each)

1. How much money is left?

   A little.

2. How much homework do we have?

   _____

3. How many students are there?

   _____

4. How much sugar do you want?

   _____

5. How many people attended the meeting?

   _____

6. How much butter do you need?

   _____

C. Fill in the blanks with gerunds. (2 points each)

1. Her brother goes *(bowl)* _bowling_ .
2. Do you enjoy *(read)* _____ books?
3. Their sister hates *(fly)* _____ .
4. My dad likes *(meet)* _____ my new teachers.
5. We just finished *(do)* _____ our homework.

Vocabulary

D. Match the expressions of quantity with the food items. (1 point each)

__d__ 1. a loaf of   a. cookies

_____ 2. a head of   b. onions

_____ 3. a bunch of   c. milk

_____ 4. a box of   d. bread

_____ 5. a gallon of   e. grapes

_____ 6. a bag of   f. lettuce

E. Fill in the missing letters. (2 points each)

1. s _h_ o _p_ _p_ ing
2. v __ l l e __ b __ l __
3. __ u __ n __ n g
4. g __ m __ a __ t __ __ s
5. r __ __ d i __ g
6. b __ k i __ g

Communication

F. Write the correct question to each answer. Choose from the box. (2 points each)

> How many hours do you watch TV a day?
> How many kinds of fruit do you eat every day?
> How much are the CDs?
> How much water do you drink each day?

1. A: _How many kinds of fruit do you eat every day?_

   B: I eat two or more.

2. A: _____

   B: They are $15.00 each.

3. A: _____

   B: Eight or more glasses a day.

4. A: _____

   B: Two hours a day.

SONG

BBMak

To gain attention, BBMak (Christian Burns, Mark Barry, and Stephen McNally) gave free performances outside the buildings of record companies. They also put on their own show and invited record companies to attend. The approach worked. Today the band is internationally famous. Their first single, "Back Here," topped the charts in 2000.

Back Here

Baby set me free
From this misery
I can't take it no more
Since you ran away
Nothing's been the same
Don't know what I'm living for
Here I am, so alone
And there's nothing in this world I can do

Chorus

Until you're back here, baby
Miss you, want you, need you so
Until you're back here, baby, yeah
There's a feeling inside I want you to know
You are the one and I can't let you go

So I told you lies
Even made you cry
Baby, I was so wrong
Girl, I promise you
Now my love is true
This is where my heart belongs
'Cos here I am, so alone
And there's nothing in this world I can do

Repeat chorus

And I wonder
Are you thinking of me
'Cos I'm thinking of you
And I wonder
Are you ever coming back in my life
'Cos here I am, so alone
And there's nothing in this world I can do

Repeat chorus

1. ∩ Listen and read the song. Why is the person in the song unhappy?

2. Work with a partner. In your notebook, rewrite the lines below using correct, grammatical English.
   - I can't take it no more.
   - Miss you, want you, need you.
   - 'Cos here I am, so alone.

3. Pretend you are the person in the song. In your notebook, write a letter to someone asking him or her to "come back" to you. Use some of the phrases from the song in your letter.

GAME *Game Show Quiz*

1. Play in pairs. Player 1 covers the Player 2 Question Set with a piece of paper. Player 2 covers the Player 1 Question Set.
2. Player 1 looks at the scoreboard and picks a category and number of points to try for. For example, "Food for 10."
3. Player 2 asks the question from his or her question set ("Can you cook?"). Player 1 answers, "Yes, I can" or "No, I can't." If player 1 gives the appropriate answer, he or she circles the selected number on the scoreboard. If Player 1 cannot answer appropriately, he or she crosses that number off the scoreboard.
4. Player 2 picks a category and number of points. Players continue taking turns.
5. At the end of the game, the player who circled the most points wins.

Player 1				Score Board	Player 2			
Food	10	20	30	Sports	10	20	30
People	10	20	30	Drinks	10	20	30
Free Time	10	20	30	Entertainment	10	20	30

Player 1 Question Set

Sports
10 Can you windsurf?
20 Do you like going to baseball games?
30 How often do you go swimming?

Drinks
10 What's your favorite drink?
20 Is soda good for you?
30 How much water do you drink each day?

Entertainment
10 Do you like going to concerts?
20 How often do you go to the movies?
30 What does your favorite singer look like?

Player 2 Question Set

Food
10 Can you cook?
20 What are pizzas topped with?
30 How many servings of vegetables do you eat each day?

People
10 How old is your mother?
20 Where is your father from?
30 What does your best friend look like?

Free Time
10 Do you like listening to music?
20 What do you do after school?
30 What do you like doing on weekends?

5 He's reading.

Learning Goals

Communication
Talk about activities that are happening right now

Grammar
Present continuous: information questions
Simple present and the present continuous

Vocabulary
Leisure activities

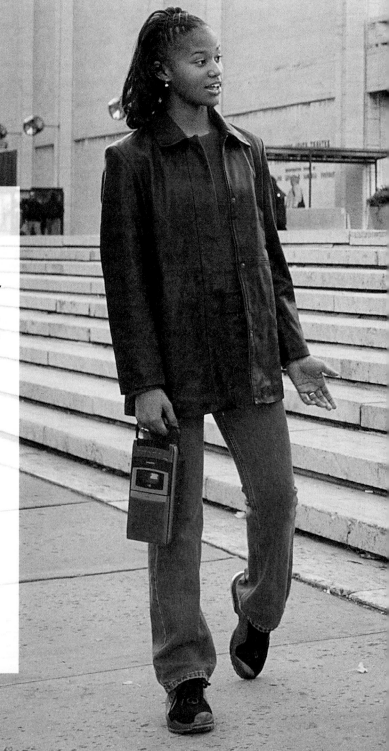

1 Dialogue

🎧 **Listen and read. Who is a bookworm?**

Karen: Hi, Diane. Are you waiting for me?

Diane: Well, yeah, Karen. You're late again, as usual.

Karen: I'm sorry. I didn't know what to wear. So what are the others doing? Are they here yet?

Diane: Of course they are. I just checked. They're waiting for us in the auditorium. Alex is practicing the songs on his guitar. Paul is coaching him.

Karen: Is Joe there, too?

Diane: Yeah. He's hanging out backstage. He's reading, I think.

Karen: Joe reads everywhere. He's such a bookworm. Tell him to get a life.

Diane: Why don't you tell him?

Karen: Nah, forget it. Come on. Let's go.

Diane: Hey, wait up! You're walking too fast.

Karen: Well, everybody's waiting for us, right?

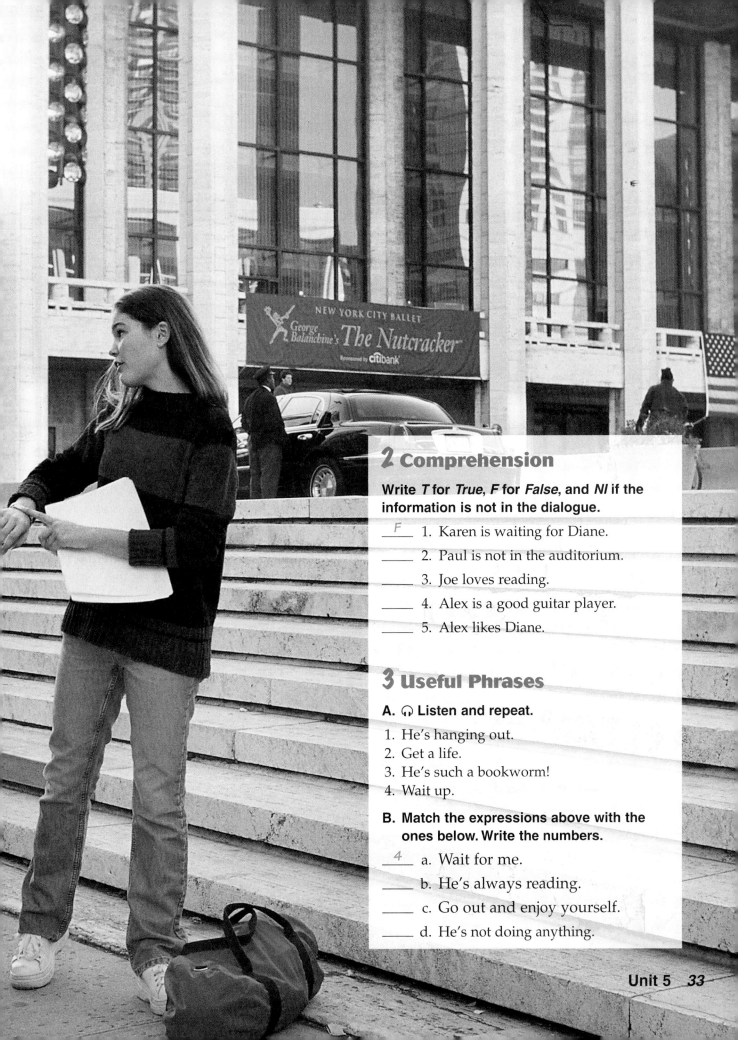

2 Comprehension

Write *T* for *True*, *F* for *False*, and *NI* if the information is not in the dialogue.

___F___ 1. Karen is waiting for Diane.

_____ 2. Paul is not in the auditorium.

_____ 3. Joe loves reading.

_____ 4. Alex is a good guitar player.

_____ 5. Alex likes Diane.

3 Useful Phrases

A. 🎧 Listen and repeat.

1. He's hanging out.
2. Get a life.
3. He's such a bookworm!
4. Wait up.

B. Match the expressions above with the ones below. Write the numbers.

___4___ a. Wait for me.

_____ b. He's always reading.

_____ c. Go out and enjoy yourself.

_____ d. He's not doing anything.

GRAMMAR FOCUS

The present continuous

Information questions

Wh- word	be	subject	verb + ing
What	**are**	you	**doing**?
Why	**is**	he	**singing**?
Where	**is**	she	**sitting**?

Who (Subject) be		verb + ing
Who	**is**	**singing**?

Long answers

Subject	verb + ing
I	**am studying**.
He	**is singing** because he's happy.
She	**is sitting** next to the director.

Subject	verb + ing
Alex	**is singing**.

Remember! Use the present continuous to express an action that is happening right now.

4 Vocabulary

Leisure activities

Look at the picture below. Who is doing each activity? Write the names.

Mark, Elena jogging

_____ flying a kite

_____ relaxing

_____ taking photographs

_____ playing board games

_____ playing volleyball

5 Practice

A. Fill in the blanks with the present continuous form of the verbs in parentheses.

1. Alice *(relax)* _is relaxing_ at the park.

2. Jim and Michael *(play)* _____ volleyball.

3. Andy *(fly)* _____ a kite.

4. Kevin *(take)* _____ a photograph.

5. Elena and Mark *(jog)* _____ .

B. In your notebook, write four different kinds of information questions for the sentences in Exercise A.

Where is Alice relaxing? _____

The simple present and the present continuous

Simple present	Present continuous
I **watch** the news regularly.	I **am watching** it right now.
Alex **plays** the guitar every day.	He **is playing** his guitar right now.
We **study** every day.	We **are studying** right now.
What **does** she **do** in her free time?	What **is** she **doing** right now?
What **do** they **do** every weekend?	What **are** they **doing** right now?

6 Information Gap

Student A, go to page 91. Student B, go to page 92. Follow the instructions.

7 Practice

Read Paul's journal. Fill in the blanks with either the present continuous or the simple present. You may use contractions.

October 19

Every year at this time, Teen Scenes (1. put) _puts_ on a variety show. Right now, I (2. sit) _____ in the director's chair, and I (3. watch) _____ the performers rehearse. I enjoy every one of these kids. Their personalities are so different! Alex always (4. arrive) _____ an hour ahead of everybody. Right now, he (5. play) _____ his guitar and (6. practice) _____ his songs. Joe does the lights, and he's the group's bookworm. He (7. read) _____ every day, everywhere. Right now, he (8. read) _____ in a corner. Diane, Lori, and Karen (9. talk) _____. These girls always have something to talk about. Wait a minute. Diane seems upset. Is she crying?

8 Your Turn

In your notebook, write a journal entry similar to Paul's. Describe what three of your classmates are doing. What do they usually do at this time?

9 Communication

Talking about activities that are happening now

🎧 Listen and read. Then role-play the conversation.

A: Hey, what are you doing right now?
B: I'm reading a book.
A: You're reading a book? Wow! You usually play video games in your free time.

10 Listening

🎧 Listen to Paul's phone call. Circle the correct answer.

1. Leo is in _____.
   a. New York   (b.) Michigan   c. Chicago
2. Paul and Leo are talking about a _____.
   a. sports event   b. theater event
   c. rock concert
3. Leo works at a _____.
   a. bank   b. high school
   c. university
4. He's looking for someone who can sing and _____.
   a. dance   b. write scripts
   c. act
5. Leo needs a _____ performer.
   a. child   b. female   c. male

11 Reading

A. Read the article about George Vlosich.

Forever Sketching

Ask George Vlosich the question, "What are you doing?" His answer will likely be, "I'm sketching." Yes, George Vlosich loves sketching. His tool? Etch-a-Sketch™, a popular children's drawing toy.

George's house is like a museum. There are sketches and pictures of George with famous people like athlete Michael Jordan. One picture is of former U.S. president Bill Clinton and former vice-president Al Gore next to George. George sketched their portraits, and the two U.S. leaders signed them.

Because of his unique talent, George is a popular guest on Nickelodeon and other TV shows. Recently, he appeared on *Ripley's Believe It or Not*.

Now in college, George is studying the visual arts. And yes, he is still sketching and having fun with his Etch-a-Sketch.

B. Circle the answers.

1. To sketch is to _____.
   a. write   (b.) draw   c. paint
2. A sketch is a _____.
   a. black-and-white drawing
   b. colorful painting
   c. photograph
3. Another word for *popular* is _____.
   a. beautiful   b. rich   c. well liked
4. *Unique* means _____.
   a. special   b. common   c. ordinary
5. People go to museums to _____.
   a. see exhibits   b. see sports events
   c. watch plays

12 Listening

A. Look up the meanings of these words.

1. drill   4. powder
2. hole   5. glue
3. empty   6. open

B. ∩ Now listen to the audio. Fill in the blanks to complete the instructions.

1. First, ___*drill*___ holes in the back of the screen.
2. Or carefully _____ the plastic case.
3. Then _____ the extra powder from the back of the Etch-a-Sketch.
4. Finally, _____ the case back on.

Learn to Learn

Learning how to spell some words

You need to know how to spell certain verbs when you use them in the present continuous. Here are two spelling rules to follow:

- For one-syllable words with a consonant, a vowel, and a consonant (CVC), double the last consonant and add *–ing*. For example, *jog – jogging*.

  But do not double the last consonant if it is *w*, *x*, or *y*. For example, *mix – mixing*.

- If a verb ends in a silent *e*, drop the final *e* and add *–ing*. For example, *smile – smiling*.

On the Phone with Alex

🎧 **Listen and read. Then discuss this question: Lori knows that Diane likes Alex. Is it right for Lori to say yes right away? Why or why not?**

1

Hi, Diane. It's Alex. What are you doing right now?

Not much. Why? Hey, what's all that noise? Where are you?

2

I'm near Madison Square Garden. Listen, where's everybody?

Who? Joe? He's here. He's with Lori. They're doing their homework. By the way, Alex, I'm planning . . .

3

Lori's there? I'm sorry. What are you planning to do?

Well, I'm planning to go to the movies. Do you want to come?

4

Sure. Is Lori going to come? Can I talk to her?

What for?

5

So I can ask her if she wants to come with us.

Oh, OK. Lori, it's for you.

6

Hi, Lori. Diane and I are planning to go to the movies today. Would you like to come?

Sure. I'd love to. What time?

6 What are you going to wear?

1 Vocabulary

Clothes

🎧 **Look at the pictures and the list of clothing items.**
Listen and point to each clothing item as it is mentioned.

- cap
- hat
- dress
- jacket
- gloves
- jeans
- T-shirt
- sweater
- coat
- tights
- pants
- skirt
- top
- sandals
- sneakers
- windbreaker
- shoes
- socks
- boots
- scarf
- sweatshirt

Melissa

Scott

Bruce

2 Practice

Take note of what some of your classmates are wearing. Then sit face-to-face with a partner. Take turns describing what a classmate is wearing and guessing who it is.

A: She's wearing a red top, jeans, white sneakers, and eyeglasses. Who is it?

B: Louise. My turn. He's wearing a white T-shirt, black pants, and black sneakers. He's not wearing socks. Who is it?

Terry

3 Communication

Commenting, complimenting, and responding to a compliment

A. ⌒ Listen and read.

A: What do you think of this dress?

B: Hmm. I'm not sure I like it. I think it's too short.

A: How about these jeans?

B: They're great! You look good in them.

A: Thanks!

B. Comment on the clothing as in the examples above. Use the descriptions below the pictures.

too low

too high

too long

too short

too loose

too tight

too big

too small

4 Your Turn

Bring in magazine pictures of clothes that you like. Work in small groups and make a collage of the clothes. Share your collage with the class.

5 Dialogue

🎧 **Listen and read.**

Diane: How do I look? Be honest.

Karen: Hmm . . . try a different top. Hey, how about that cute purple top and those jeans?

Diane: That top is too tight, and those jeans are too low. What are *you* going to wear?

Karen: I'm going to wear a red miniskirt, a black top, and boots. Eat your heart out, Britney Spears.

Diane: Right! Now, let's get back to me.

Karen: Definitely, wear the jeans. Alex is going to notice you for sure.

Diane: Oh, yeah? Alex is going to notice Lori. That much I know.

Karen: Oooh . . . you're jealous!

Diane: I am not! Hey, is that the phone ringing? Mom, if it's Alex, I'm going to take it in my room.

6 Comprehension

Read the dialogue again.

1. Circle the clothes Karen wants Diane to wear.
2. Underline the clothes Karen is going to wear.

GRAMMAR FOCUS

Simple future: *be going to*

Affirmative and negative statements

Subject	*be (not)*	*going to*	base form	
I	am			
She	is (not)	going to	study	tonight.
We	are			

7 Practice

A. Look at the to-do list below. Put a check (✔) before things you are going to do after school; put an (✗) before things you are not going to do.

_____ study for tomorrow's test

_____ do homework

_____ phone a classmate

_____ watch TV

_____ read a book

_____ hang out with friends

_____ clean my room

_____ shop

B. In your notebook, write three things from the list above that you are going to do tonight and three things that you are not going to do.

I'm going to do my homework.

8 Practice

Play a fortune-telling game. Go to page 88 for instructions.

GRAMMAR FOCUS

Information questions with *be going to*

Who	**is**	he	**going to**	call?
What	**is**	she	**going to**	do?
Where	**is**	it	**going to**	be?
When	**are**	you	**going to**	visit?
How	**are**	we	**going to**	do	it?

9 Pronunciation

The sound of *going to* + verb

A. ⌒ Listen and repeat.

1. I'm going to talk to her.
2. They're going to play.
3. We're going to practice.
4. She's going to wear that shirt.

B. ⌒ Listen and repeat.

A: What are you going to wear to the party tonight?
B: I'm going to wear jeans and a T-shirt. What about you?

10 Practice

A. Work with a partner. Look at the pictures below. Write what's going to happen next. Use *be going to*.

1. man/catch/woman
   The man is going to catch the woman.

2. clown/slip/on the banana peel
   _____

3. woman acrobat/fall
   _____

4. man/wake up
   _____

5. man/miss the bus
   _____

B. In your notebook, write questions for the sentences in Exercise A. Use the cues.

1. What/happen/woman
   What is going to happen to the woman?
2. Why/clown/slip
3. What/happen
4. Why/man/wake up
5. Who/be late/for work

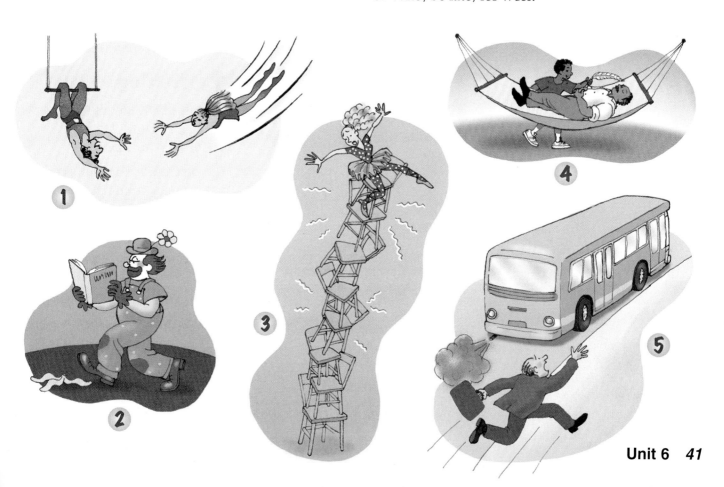

11 Reading

This is a timed reading activity. Before you read, follow your teacher's instructions.

Life Is a Circus

As a child, Sonia told her mom, "Someday, I'm going to join the circus." Today, 14-year-old Sonia is living a childhood dream. Sonia is a performer with the Cirque du Soleil, a world-famous performing group.

Here's Sonia's story:

"I liked acrobatics as a child. I started gymnastics at the National Circus School when I was four. At the circus school, I learned acrobatics, juggling, trampoline, and floor vaults. When I was eleven, Cirque du Soleil hired me. It was a dream come true.

Circus life is not easy. It is a life of discipline. I always make sure that I plan my daily activities. Today is a typical day. I am in school from 9 A.M. to 3 P.M. After school, I am going to practice on the trapeze from 4 to 6 P.M. I am going to have dinner at 7 and perform from 8 to 11 P.M. My schedule seems too busy for most people, but I like it.

Overall, life on the road is difficult. I'm always away from my family and friends. But I like traveling and making new friends. Best of all, I love performing for 2,500 people a night. It's a unique experience."

12 Comprehension

Answer the questions as fast as you can.

1. How old is Sonia? _____14_____

2. What performing group hired Sonia? _____

3. What four things did Sonia learn at the National Circus School? _____, _____, _____, and _____.

4. List the activity Sonia does at each time given below:

   _____ 9 A.M.–3 P.M.

   _____ 4 P.M.–6 P.M.

   _____ 8 P.M.–11 P.M.

13 Speaking

In groups of three, discuss these questions:

1. Why is life at the circus difficult?
2. Why is life at the circus fun?
3. What does Sonia like most about working at the circus?

14 Listening

🎧 Listen to a radio ad for circus applicants. Write *T* for *True*, *F* for *False*.

_T_ 1. Cirque du Soleil is a performing group.

____ 2. It needs teachers.

____ 3. Applicants should send their applications to Canada.

____ 4. Cirque de Soleil has a website.

____ 5. Applicants should not send in videotapes with their applications.

Progress Check *Units 5 and 6*

Grammar

A. Write information questions about the underlined words. Use *who, why, what, where,* **and** *when.* **(2 points each)**

1. <u>Mark</u> is playing video games.
   Who is playing video games?

2. The baby is crying <u>because he's hungry</u>.
   _____

3. They are <u>eating dinner</u> right now.
   _____

4. I'm going to play <u>in the park</u>.
   _____

5. Beth is <u>doing her homework</u>.
   _____

B. Circle the correct form of the verb to complete each sentence. (2 points each)

1. He *(is speaking/speaks)* two languages: English and Japanese.
2. They *(travel/are traveling)* every summer.
3. It's a great party! *(Are you enjoying/Do you enjoy)* it?
4. Be quiet! I *(am studying/study)* for my exam.
5. Mom *(is making/makes)* dinner in the kitchen right now.
6. Tetsuo *(is getting/gets)* up at six o'clock every day.

C. Read the statements. Then write a sentence with *be going to* **and the words in parentheses. (2 points each)**

1. Look at those dark clouds! *(rain)*
   It's going to rain.

2. My hands are dirty. *(wash)*
   _____

3. Her room is very messy. *(clean)*
   _____

4. We just missed the bus. *(be late for class)*
   _____

5. The kids are hungry. *(eat a snack)*
   _____

Vocabulary

D. What can you wear for the following activities? Write three or four clothing items from pages 38-39 under each column. (1 point each)

Painting	Gardening	Partying
T-shirt	gloves	mini skirt

Communication

E. Circle the correct response for each question or statement. (2 points each)

1. Look at my new sunglasses!
   a. Definitely wear it!
   b. They're great!
2. How do I look in these jeans?
   a. They're too low.
   b. You're jealous!
3. What do you think of these shoes?
   a. They're too short.
   b. I think they're cool.
4. What do you think of these boots?
   a. I'm not sure I like them.
   b. Sure. I'd love to.
5. How do I look?
   a. Yes. You look good in them.
   b. You look great!

Wide Angle on the world

1 Reading

A. Scan the article quickly. In paragraph 2, circle what skateboarders can do. Then read the article carefully.

B. Work with a partner. Take turns explaining to each other the meanings of the words below. You can draw or act out the meanings.

1. zoom upward
2. twist
3. turn
4. bend
5. drop in
6. lean forward

C. Look at the picture of a skateboard. Label the three basic parts.

tail

D. Work with a partner. In your notebook, write the five major steps for doing the ollie.

1. _Hit the tail part of your skateboard with your back foot._

2 Listening

🎧 Listen to the announcement. Then write *T* for *True* or *F* for *False*.

__T__ 1. There will be a skateboarding exhibition at the Exploratorium.

____ 2. The exhibition is on June 12.

____ 3. Tim Piumarta is a professional skateboarder.

____ 4. Paul Doherty will explain the science of skateboarding.

____ 5. Paul Doherty is a physicist.

____ 6. Tickets are available at the ticket booth.

3 Speaking

Work with a partner. Ask each other questions about a favorite sport or game.

A: Which do you like better, skateboarding or in-line skating?
B: I like in-line skating better. It's not as exciting as skateboarding, but it's safer. How about you?

The Thrill of Skateboarding

- **The trucks:** The trucks connect the wheels to the deck and allow the board to turn.
- **The wheels:** The wheels affect the smoothness and speed of the ride.
- **The bearings:** The bearings enable the wheels to turn.

Watching skateboarder Tony Hawk is an amazing experience. On his skateboard, Hawk zooms upward, twists, and turns—all at top speed and way up in the air. How does he do it? Is the skateboard attached to his feet?

In the beginning, skateboarding was simple. Skateboarders skated on streets or sidewalks. Their most exciting trick was to slide down the top of a hill. Today's skateboarders are like flying acrobats. They leap, skid over obstacles, flip, and turn at amazing speeds. What secret powers do these skateboarders have? Doesn't gravity apply to them? The answer is simple: understand the laws of physics.

THE PARTS OF A SKATEBOARD

A skateboard has many different parts, but the four basic parts are:

- The board or deck: The deck is made of several sheets of maple wood, which are glued together. The back of the board is called the tail.

TWO SKATEBOARDING TRICKS

THE OLLIE

The ollie is basically jumping with the board. Here's how to do the ollie: First, hit the tail part of your skateboard really hard with your back foot, and then slide your front foot up at the same time. These moves pop the board up in the air. When in the air, keep at the center of the board and then land with your feet spread out. Bend your knees as you are landing.

DROPPING INTO A HALF PIPE

Dropping in is moving from the top of a ramp into the ramp itself. To do this, put your board or the tail part of your board on top of the ramp, so the board is hanging over the edge. Your back foot should be on the tail, and your front foot toward the front of the board. With the board in position, lean forward and skate down the ramp. Remember, the main technique of dropping in is the leaning forward.

Want more tricks? Go to http://www.sk8uk.co.uk or http://www.exploratorium.edu/skateboarding. Have fun!

7

You were awesome, Alex!

Learning Goals

Communication
Talk about past events
Agree or disagree with someone

Grammar
Simple past: regular verbs

Vocabulary
Past-time markers

1 Dialogue

🎧 **Listen and read. Was Green Fire's performance good?**

Lori: You were awesome, Alex!

Alex: Thanks. Green Fire was great, too. In fact, you were wonderful on stage.

Diane: Congratulations, Alex! You were great.

Alex: Thanks, Diane. Lori liked my performance, too.

Diane: Oh.

Alex: So where did you learn to dance like that?

Diane: We watched a lot of MTV videos and borrowed ideas from other groups.

Lori: Not really, Diane. We created our own dance moves. Remember?

Diane: You're right, Lori. We did.

Alex: I can believe that. So Lori, are you going to the party later? Can I pick you up?

Lori: Thanks, but my dad's dropping me off.

Diane: You can go to the party with Joe and me, Alex. Oh, hi, Paul.

Paul: That was a great show, guys. Congratulations. Umm . . . . Alex, can I talk to you for a minute?

2 Comprehension

Identify the person or people in the dialogue.

Lori, Diane 1. Two members of Green Fire.

_____ 2. Alex values her opinion a lot.

_____ 3. He wants to attend the party with Lori.

_____ 4. She wants Alex to be with her at the party.

3 Useful Phrases

A. 🎧 **Listen and read.**

- Not really./I don't agree.
- You're right./I agree.

B. Complete the dialogue below with expressions from Exercise A. Then role-play the situation.

A: Do you like _Gilmore Girls_? I love it. It's a great show.

B: _____. I think it's boring.

C: _____.

4 Vocabulary

Past-time markers

A. 🎧 **Listen and repeat.**

yesterday	a week ago	last night
yesterday morning	a month ago	last year

B. Look at the calendar below. Use the circled day as your point of reference to answer the questions. Write the dates on the lines.

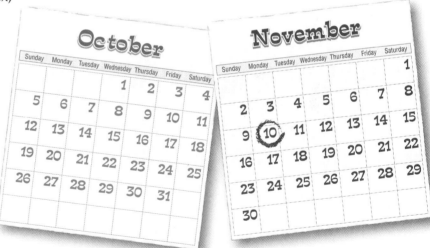

November 3 1. What day was a week ago?

_____ 2. What day was yesterday morning?

_____ 3. When was a month ago?

_____ 4. What day was last night?

_____ 5. What year was last year? (Use the current year as a point of reference.)

GRAMMAR FOCUS

The simple past tense: regular verbs

Affirmative statements

I **sneezed** a lot
He **stayed** home
We **studied**
They **hugged**
} last night.

Yes/No questions

Did you **sneeze**
Did he **stay**
Did we **study**
Did they **hug**
} last night?

Negative statements

I **did not** sneeze
He **did not stay** home
We **did not study**
They **did not hug**
} last night.

Answers

Yes, I **did**. *Or* No, I **didn't**.
Yes, he **did**. *Or* No, he **didn't**.
Yes, we **did**. *Or* No, we **didn't**.
Yes, they **did**. *Or* No, they **didn't**.

5 Practice

Have a competition. Go to page 89.

6 Practice

A. Work with a partner. Complete the questionnaire below for yourself. Then ask your partner the questions.

B. In your notebook, write sentences stating four things your partner did and four things your partner did *not* do. Use the information in the questionnaire.

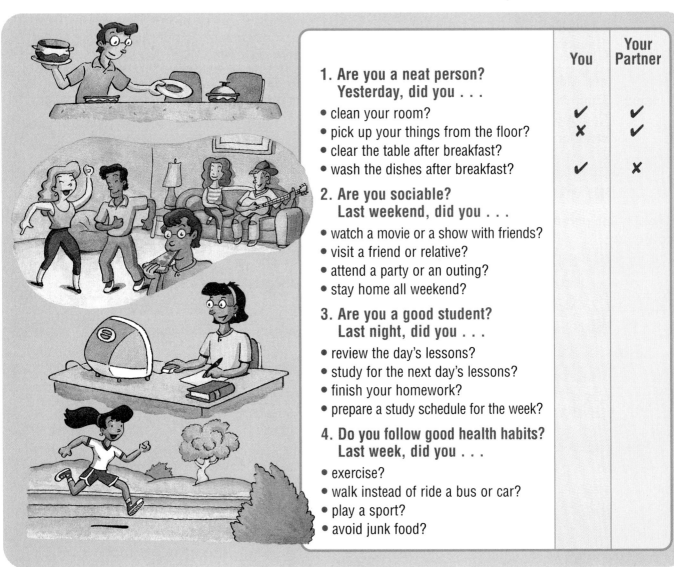

	You	Your Partner
1. Are you a neat person? Yesterday, did you . . .		
• clean your room?	✔	✔
• pick up your things from the floor?	✗	✔
• clear the table after breakfast?		
• wash the dishes after breakfast?	✔	✗
2. Are you sociable? Last weekend, did you . . .		
• watch a movie or a show with friends?		
• visit a friend or relative?		
• attend a party or an outing?		
• stay home all weekend?		
3. Are you a good student? Last night, did you . . .		
• review the day's lessons?		
• study for the next day's lessons?		
• finish your homework?		
• prepare a study schedule for the week?		
4. Do you follow good health habits? Last week, did you . . .		
• exercise?		
• walk instead of ride a bus or car?		
• play a sport?		
• avoid junk food?		

7 Practice

Fill in the blanks with the simple past form of the verbs.

Mom: Joe, I think you have something to explain to us.

Diane: Yeah, Joe. What's your story?

Joe: Be quiet, Diane. I'm sorry I was out late last night, Mom. I *(1. miss)* ___missed___ my stop because I was reading on the bus. I *(2. end)* _____ up at a garage.

Diane: So what *(3. happen)* _____ next?

Joe: I *(4. check)* _____ my wallet. There was no money in it.

Diane: You're a hopeless case, Joe. Then?

Joe: I *(5. walk)* _____ for miles. I *(6. knock)* _____ on the door of the first house with lights on. A nice lady *(7. open)* _____ the door. I *(8. explain)* _____ my situation. Her husband *(9. call)* _____ a taxi and handed me $20. I have their phone number.

Mom: That was nice of them. Let's call these people and thank them.

The simple past tense: information questions

Wh- word	*did*	subject	main verb	Answers
Who	**did**	you	**help**?	The principal.
Where	**did**	they	**stay**?	At a hotel.
When	**did**	he	**arrive**?	Last night.
Why	**did**	we	**fail**?	Because we didn't study.

8 Practice

Work with a partner. Write four information questions about the dialogue using the simple past form.

1. What happened/Joe
   What happened to Joe last night?

2. Why/miss his stop
   _____

3. Where/end up
   _____

4. Who/help/Joe
   _____

5. What/the husband/do
   _____

9 Listening

🎧 Look at the fashion timeline below. Then listen to the conversation. Write the clothes each person is wearing under the correct year.

	1950s	1960s	1970s
Mom		*bell bottoms*	
Mom's friend			
Aunt Mildred			
Grandma			

10 Reading

Which of the clothes below are in fashion again?

11 Your Turn

In the timeline below, write descriptions of clothes currently in fashion. Find pictures and show them to the class. Then discuss these questions:

1. What is your favorite decade in terms of fashion? Why?
2. What decade do you think has the worst fashion? Why?

Learn to Learn

Learning meanings of new words through pictures

In the fashion timeline, you learned several new words related to clothes. One way of learning the meanings of words is to look at pictures or drawings that go with the words.

Fashion timeline

1950s

motorcycle jackets
Bermuda shorts
pedal pushers

1960s

miniskirts
T-shirts with peace signs
"go-go" boots
bell bottoms
big hairdos

1990s

designer athletic shoes
puffy jackets
baggy pants

1980s

designer jeans; boots
the "Madonna" look
big jewelry
big hairdos

1970s

Western boots
denim jeans
pantsuits

Present

_____
_____
_____

The Good News

A. 🎧 **Listen and read. What is Paul's good news?**

Paul, did you want to see me? Did I do something wrong?

Oh, no. In fact, I have good news.

Good news? What is it?

I'm going to recommend you to a performing arts program at the University of Michigan.

Wow! Why me, Paul?

Because I think you're very talented. So what do you think?

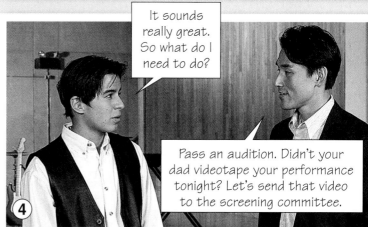

It sounds really great. So what do I need to do?

Pass an audition. Didn't your dad videotape your performance tonight? Let's send that video to the screening committee.

I can't believe this. I want to call my dad. Thanks, Paul! You just made my day.

It's not a done deal, Alex. Remember, there's still an audition.

B. Discuss these questions: What sentence tells you that Alex has a close relationship with his father? If you received a scholarship, who would you tell first?

8 Did you hear the news?

Learning Goals

Communication
Talk about past events
Express opinion

Grammar
Simple past: irregular verbs
Conjunctions: *and, but, so*

Vocabulary
Adjectives to describe states of being and feelings

1 Vocabulary

A. 🎧 Listen and repeat.

happy	sad	angry
excited	nervous	tired
surprised	upset	worried

B. Now look at the pictures. Write the adjectives under the correct pictures. Try to use each adjective only once.

① _____happy_____

② _____

③ _____

④ _____

⑤ _____

⑥ _____

⑦ _____

⑧ _____

⑨ _____

2 Practice

Have a competition! Go to page 89 and follow the instructions.

3 Listening

🎧 **Listen and identify the following:**

1. The person Alex called: _____His dad_____

2. When the performing arts event will be held: _____

3. The school hosting the summer program:

    _____

4. What Alex needs for his audition:

    _____

4 Practice

Have a competition! Go to page 89 and follow the instructions.

5 Practice

Fill in the blanks with the simple past tense.

Dear Diary,

I'm so excited. This morning, I (1. have) _had_ my first riding lesson. Riding lessons are not cheap, so I (2. get) _____ a job babysitting after school to help pay for them. My mom (3. drive) _____ me to the stable, and I (4. be) _____ a little nervous. I (5. feel) _____ better when I met Amy, my instructor. She (6. tell) _____ me not to worry. She (7. bring) _____ a beautiful horse out of the barn. I (8. stand) _____ on a wooden step and learned how to get on and off the horse safely. Then we (9. go) _____ into the ring. Amy (10. teach) _____ me to walk and trot on the horse. I can't wait for my second lesson!

6 Practice

Sit in a circle with five classmates. Follow your teacher's instructions.

Tracy: I went to the movies last Saturday.

Elinore: Tracy went to the movies last Saturday. I read a book.

Anthony: Tracy went to the movies last Saturday. Elinore read a book.

7 Practice

In your notebook, rewrite the affirmative sentences below into negative ones. Use contractions.

1. I went to school yesterday.

    I didn't go to school yesterday.

2. I took a shower after gym class.

3. I slept well last night.

4. I had breakfast this morning.

5. I was at home last weekend.

6. We were absent last Friday.

8 Dialogue

🎧 **Read and listen.**
What is Lori's reaction to the news about Alex?

Joe: What's up, Alex? You look excited. Are you and Lori . . . ?

Alex: No, it's not about Lori. OK. Here's the news, but don't tell anyone yet. Paul recommended me for a summer program at the University of Michigan.

Joe: Wow. The University of Michigan! Hey, Lori. Did you hear the news? Paul recommended Alex to the University of Michigan. Alex is going there this summer. Can you believe that?

Alex: Oh man. Joe, I told you not to tell anyone. I still need to audition. Hi, Lori.

Lori: Hi. That's news to me, Alex. When did Paul tell you this?

Alex: Just now, after the show.

Lori: I see. I have to go. Bye.

Alex: Wait. Lori, are you coming to the party?

Lori: I'm not sure. I'm not feeling well. Maybe.

9 Comprehension

Answer the questions orally.

1. Why is Alex excited?
2. When did Paul tell Alex about the recommendation?
3. Is Lori happy about the news? Underline the part in the dialogue that proves your answer.

10 Communication

Expressing opinion

🎧 **Listen and read. Then role-play the situation.**

Karen: Hi, Lori. Hey, are you all right?

Lori: I'm upset about Paul, Karen. I think he was unfair to us. I think he was wrong not to tell us about the summer program at the University of Michigan.

Karen: Don't be upset, Lori. I'm sure Paul had a good reason. Let's go talk to him.

GRAMMAR FOCUS

Conjunctions: *and, but, so*

She is my friend, **and** I like her.
I am tired, **but** I can't sleep.
Julia passed the test, **so** she called her mom.

> **Remember!** Use conjunctions and a comma (,) to join two sentences.

And adds information to the idea.
But adds a contrast.
So expresses a result.

11 Practice

Fill in the blanks with *and*, *but*, or *so*. Add a comma (,) before each conjunction.

1. Alex is a good performer, ___so___ Paul recommended him for the summer program.

2. Lori is also a good performer _____ Paul did not recommend her.

3. Alex wants to go to the summer program _____ he has to pass the audition first.

4. Alex is close to his dad _____ Alex told him about the exciting news first.

5. Alex is excited about the news _____ Joe is excited, too.

6. Joe told Lori the news about Alex _____ she became upset.

12 Practice

The sentence pairs below summarize the events in Units 7 and 8. Join the pairs with *and*, *but*, or *so*.

1. Teen Scenes had a wonderful show this year. Alex put on a great performance.

   Teen Scenes had a wonderful show this
   year, and Alex put on a great performance.

2. Leo needed an actor and musician. He called Paul for a recommendation.

   _____

   _____

3. Alex was happy about the recommendation. He was nervous about the audition.

   _____

   _____

4. Joe was excited for Alex. Lori was not excited for him.

   _____

   _____

13 Reading

A. Read Sarah's diary entry. Underline the sentences that express what friendship is.

December 10

Dear Diary,

Monica just called. She said she was with Emily, so she couldn't come over today. Monica was my best friend. We grew up together. We're very much alike: we like the same things, and we even think alike. When I was with Monica, I could be myself. She made everything OK. She taught me how to feel good about myself, and we always had a good time together.

But these days, Monica spends a lot of time with Emily, and she's always comparing the two of us. I feel really sad every time Monica does this.

Fifth grade was the perfect year. Monica and I were on top of the world! Then Emily came along and took my best friend away from me.

Sarah

B. Compare the sentences you underlined. Work with a classmate. Did you underline the same ideas?

14 Your Turn

Work with a partner. Discuss these questions:

1. Would you advise Sarah to continue to be Monica's friend? Why or why not?
2. What do you look for in a friend? Share your ideas with the class.

15 Speaking

A. Below are the results of a survey on the top five qualities people look for in a good friend. Discuss the meanings of the words with your teacher.

B. Discuss the survey results in groups of three or four. Do you agree with the order? What would you add or delete from the list?

16 Writing

Write about your best friend. Why do you consider this person your best friend? What are his/her qualities? Share your paragraph with the class.

THE FIVE QUALITIES OF A BEST FRIEND

Chum   Friend

1 Trustworthy
2 Honest
3 Fun
4 Understanding
5 Loyal

Pal   Buddy

Progress Check *Units 7 and 8*

Grammar

A. Fill in the blanks with the simple past form of the verbs in parentheses. (2 points each)

1. I *(walk)* _walked_ to school yesterday.
2. The children *(stay)* _____ up late on New Year's Eve.
3. I *(make)* _____ dinner last night.
4. Dad *(have)* _____ coffee for breakfast.
5. The show *(be)* _____ wonderful.
6. They *(be)* _____ late this morning.

B. Rewrite the sentences to make them negative. (3 points each)

1. She knew him from high school.
   She didn't know him from high school.
2. We bought the CDs for you.
   _____
3. I met the new neighbors yesterday.
   _____
4. Paul drove to Connecticut last Saturday.
   _____
5. The students did their homework.
   _____
6. The baby slept well last night.
   _____

C. Combine each set of two sentences into one, using *and*, *but*, or *so*. (3 points each)

1. Our house is small. It's nice.
   Our house is small, but it's nice.
2. Pedro likes Rosa. He often calls her.
   _____
3. I like New York. I don't like New York weather.
   _____

4. It was very cloudy. I took my umbrella with me.
   _____
5. Joe's father is upset. His mother is upset, too.
   _____
6. Angela likes rock music. She doesn't like heavy metal.
   _____

Vocabulary

D. What are these adjectives? Write the missing vowels *a*, *e*, *i*, *o*, or *u* in the blanks. (2 points each)

1. w _o_ r r _i_ _e_ d
2. s _ d
3. s _ r p r _ s _ d
4. _ n g r y
5. h _ p p y
6. t _ r _ d
7. _ p s _ t
8. n _ r v _ _ s
9. _ x c _ t _ d

Communication

E. Work with two classmates. Write a conversation about this situation: Student A thinks the movie version of *Harry Potter and the Sorcerer's Stone* is better than the book. Student B likes the book better. Student C agrees with Student B. (4 points)

SONG

Amy Grant

She made her first album, "Amy Grant", when she was only 16 years old. A five-time Grammy winner, Amy Grant is well known for the positive message of her music.

Baby, Baby

Baby, baby
I'm taken with the notion
To love you with the sweetest of devotion.
Baby, baby
My tender love will flow from
The bluest sky to the deepest ocean.

Stop for a minute
Baby, I'm so glad you're mine, yeah
You're mine.

Baby, baby
The stars are shining for you
And just like me I'm sure that they adore you.
Baby, baby
Go walking through the forest
The birds above are singing you a chorus.

Chorus

Stop for a minute
Baby, I'm so glad you're mine, oh yeah
And ever since the day you put my heart in motion
Baby I realize that there's just no getting over you.

Baby, baby
In any kind of weather
I'm here for you always and forever.
Baby, baby
No muscle man could sever
My love for you is true and it will never

Repeat chorus

1. 🎧 Work with a partner. Read the lyrics to the song. Select three difficult words and look up their meanings in a dictionary. Then listen to the song.

2. Read the lyrics again. The person in the song makes some promises to her "baby." What are they? Compare your answers with a partner.

GAME Q & A Baseball

Steps

1. Create a baseball diamond in the classroom. Choose a place in the front for home plate, then choose the places for first, second, and third bases around the room.

2. Next, form two teams. The first team comes to the front. Each player takes his or her turn at "bat."

3. The "pitcher" (your teacher) asks the "batter" a review question. If the batter answers correctly, he or she goes to first base and the other players already on the field move one base. For each player who reaches home plate, the team scores a "run." If the batter does not answer correctly, the team scores an "out."

4. Keep track of "outs" and "runs." After three outs or five minutes, whichever comes first, the second team comes to bat.

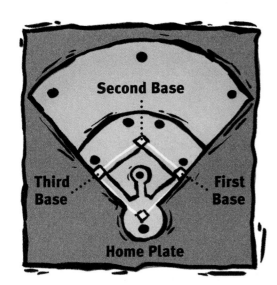

Review Questions

Unit 5

What are you doing right now?
What is _____ doing right now?
Where is _____ standing?
What do you do in your free time?

Unit 6

What are you going to wear to school tomorrow?
What time are you going to leave school today?
What are you going to do after school today?
How many hours did you study last night?

Unit 7

Did you _____ yesterday?
What did you do last weekend?
Did you clean your room this morning?
How long did you study last night?

Unit 8

What did you eat for _____ yesterday?
What time did you _____ on Saturday?
Were you _____ yesterday?
Where were you Saturday at _____ o'clock?

9

Why didn't you call us?

Learning Goals

Communication
Narrate a past event
Talk about the weather

Grammar
The past continuous with *when* and *while*
Past continuous and simple past

Vocabulary
Adjectives describing the weather

1 Vocabulary

🎧 **Listen and repeat. Then match the sentences with the pictures.**

Mexico City 1. It's sunny.

_____ 2. It's rainy.

_____ 3. It's windy.

_____ 4. It's cloudy.

_____ 5. It's foggy.

_____ 6. It's snowy.

Mexico City

Berlin

Chicago

San Francisco

Tokyo

New York

2 Communication

Talking about the weather

Work with a partner. Look at the pictures on page 60 again. Take turns asking each other questions about the weather.

A: What's the weather like in Mexico City?
B: It's sunny in Mexico City.

3 Listening

A. 🎧 Listen to the international weather report. As you listen, fill in the chart.

City	Weather	
	Today	Yesterday
Hong Kong	hot and sunny	
London		snowy
São Paulo		
Washington, D.C.		cold but sunny

B. Ask each other about the weather in the cities in the chart above.

A: What's the weather like today in Hong Kong?
B: It's sunny and hot.
A: How about yesterday?
B: Terrible. It was rainy.

GRAMMAR FOCUS

Past continuous with *when* and *while*

I **was sleeping** when Josh called. *Or*
When Josh called, I **was sleeping**.
Josh called *while* I **was sleeping**. *Or*
While I **was sleeping**, Josh called.

Remember! The past continuous describes an activity in progress at a particular time in the past. Use the **past continuous** form with the *while*-clause; the **simple past** with the *when*-clause.

4 Practice

Fill in the blanks with *when* or *while*.

1. I was running after the bus ___*when*___ I fell face down on the ground.

2. _____ Kay was carrying a tray of drinks, she slipped and dropped the tray.

3. Claire was eating corn _____ a tooth fell out.

4. John was dancing on the teacher's desk _____ the principal came in.

5. _____ James was imitating his teacher, the teacher arrived.

5 Practice

Work with a partner. Examine the actions below. Which action was in progress in the past? Which action was interrupted? In your notebook, write sentences using the cues below.

1. *When*: I / think of Charles / he / call
   I was thinking of Charles when he called.
2. *While*: Marcia / eat / the doorbell / ring
3. *When*: My cousins / have a party / their parents come home
4. *While*: Mark / use the Internet / his boss arrive
5. *When*: Carl / read / the lights go out

6 Practice

Have a competition. Go to page 90. Follow the instructions.

7 Listening

🎧 **Listen and read.**

We were walking home from a party. It wasn't raining when we left the party, so we decided to walk. We were crossing 72nd Street, when suddenly, we heard somebody call for help. We looked around and saw a man lying on the sidewalk. We were scared, but we didn't want to leave the man. We knew that he was hurt and needed help. My friend Alex called 911.

While we were waiting for the ambulance, it started to rain a little. We put a jacket over the man. When the ambulance arrived, we told the EMS worker what happened. He told us to go to the police station and report the incident.

8 Comprehension

Number the sentences in the correct order to tell the story.

_2_ They heard a cry for help.

_____ They put a jacket over the man.

_____ It started to rain.

_____ The ambulance came.

_____ The four friends were walking home from a party.

_____ Alex called 911.

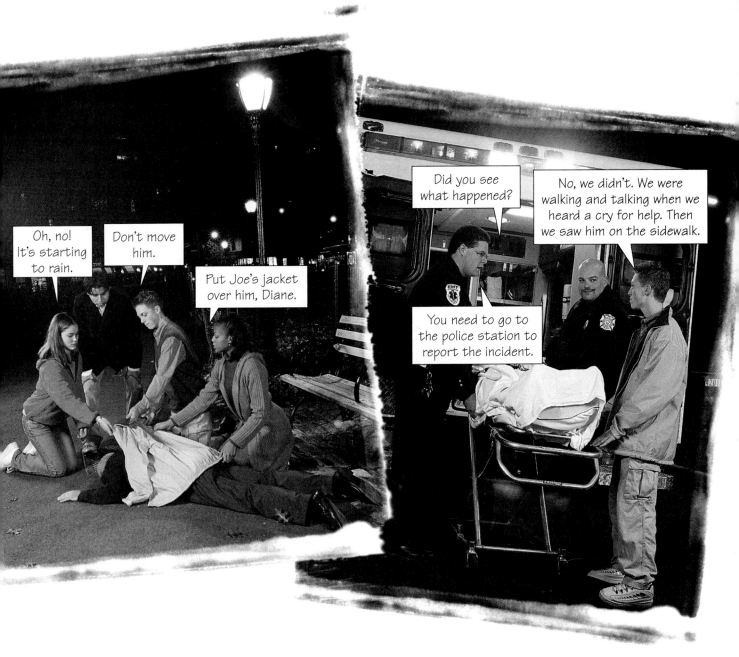

Oh, no! It's starting to rain.

Don't move him.

Put Joe's jacket over him, Diane.

Did you see what happened?

No, we didn't. We were walking and talking when we heard a cry for help. Then we saw him on the sidewalk.

You need to go to the police station to report the incident.

GRAMMAR FOCUS

The simple past contrasted with the past continuous

Simple past	Past continuous
I **slept** well last night.	At this time last night, I **was sleeping**.

Remember! Use the **simple past** for a completed action in the past.

Use the **past continuous** for an action in progress at a particular time in the past.

9 Practice

Work with a partner. Read the series of events below. Then fill in the blanks.

I (1. go) ___went___ to bed at 9:30 last night. I (2. sleep) _was sleeping_ when it (3. start) _____ to rain heavily. When I (4. wake up) _____ , my dog (5. cry) _____ next to me. He (6. shiver) _____ and (7. shake) _____ when I (8. pick) _____ him up. I (9. go) _____ out to check. The front door (10. be) _____ open. I (11. run) _____ back to bed. I was afraid.

10 Reading

Read the magazine article.

Lightning rips through teenagers' tent

Sixteen-year-old David Burren says that he and his friends are "a bunch of lucky guys," and they certainly are. One evening, David and his friends were almost struck by lightning.

David lives on a farm in Kent, England. One evening, a storm started while he and his friends were camping out behind David's house. They were inside their tent. The boys were laughing and joking when suddenly, lightning ripped through the tent. It struck a metal pole in the tent.

"It was about 1 A.M.," said David. "There was a big bang and a flash of light. Somebody shouted, 'Run, everyone, run!'" The boys ran across the field to the house. While they were running, they realized their friend Stefan was not with them.

"We went back to get Stefan. We found him in the tent. He was unconscious. We were nervous and scared. We thought he was dead," said David. "We pulled him out and put him on the grass. There were burns all over his face. While we were deciding what to do, Stefan opened his eyes and started talking about soccer! We were so relieved!" Today, David, Stefan, and their friends are making plans to celebrate their luck. David says, "We're going to have a party soon, but we're not going to camp out!"

11 Writing

A. Look at the pictures below and put the letters in the correct order to tell the story.

<u>C</u> ____ ____ ____ ____

B. Look at the pictures again. In your notebook, write a sentence about each picture, following the correct order. Use the past continuous and the simple past where possible.

David and his friends were camping out when a storm began.

Back at Home

A. 🎧 **Listen and read. Why were Diane and Joe's parents worried?**

B. Work with a partner. Diane and Joe did something good. Discuss why their parents were upset.

10 Is he better than I am?

Learning Goals

Communication
Ask and express preferences or choices: *which*

Grammar
Comparative and superlative forms of adjectives
As + adjective + *as*

Vocabulary
Adjectives

1 Dialogue

⌒ **Listen and read.**

Alex: Are you mad at me, Lori?

Lori: Should I be?

Alex: I don't know, but I think you are.

Lori: Tell me. Why did Paul choose you? Does he really think that you're the best in the group? And why didn't he tell the group about it?

Alex: I don't know why Paul chose me for the summer program in Michigan, Lori. I can't say I'm better than anyone else.

Lori: I'm sorry, Alex. I worked as hard as you did on that show, maybe even harder.

Alex: I know that, Lori. Look, you're the best singer in the group. You have a great voice. Why don't you talk to Paul? I'm sure he can explain.

Lori: Maybe later. Can we talk about something else? What time are Joe and Diane meeting us?

2 Comprehension

Work with a partner. Answer these questions:

1. Why was Lori upset?
2. What does Alex think of Lori as a singer?
3. Is Alex a good friend?

3 Useful Phrases

A. ⌒ Listen and repeat.

- Are you mad at me?
- I think you are.
- I don't know.
- Should I be?

B. Work with a partner. You think a classmate is upset with you. Write a conversation, using the phrases in Exercise A. Then role-play your conversation.

GRAMMAR FOCUS

Making comparisons with adjectives

Positive	Comparative	Superlative
short	short**er than**	**the** short**est**
big	big**ger than**	**the** big**gest**
funny	fun**nier than**	**the** fun**niest**
famous	**more** famous **than**	**the most** famous
important	**more** important **than**	**the most** important
interesting	**more** interesting **than**	**the most** interesting

Remember! Use the comparative to compare two people, two things, or two places.

Use the superlative to compare three or more people, things, or places.

4 Practice

Fill in the blanks with either the comparative or superlative form of the adjectives.

1. My bag is *heavy*.
   a. Bill's bag is ___*heavier*___ than mine.
   b. Of the three bags, Steve's bag is ___*the heaviest*___.

2. Michael Jordan is *tall*.
   a. Grant Hill is _____ than Jordan.
   b. Shaquille O'Neal is _____ of the three players.

3. A bicycle is *expensive*.
   a. A motorcycle is _____ than a bicycle.
   b. A car is _____ of the three.

4. Kate is *thin*.
   a. Rose is _____ than Kate.
   b. Kim is _____ of the three girls.

5 Practice

Look at the pictures. In your notebook, write three sentences comparing each set of pictures. Use the adjectives in the box.

| funny   exciting   old |

1. a. _Georgia is old._
   b. _Aida is older than Georgia._
   c. _Mary is the oldest of the three._

② Sports

rock climbing

bungee jumping

para sailing

① Women

Mary

Georgia

Aida

③ Actors

Eddie Murphy

Will Smith

Jim Carrey

6 Practice

Have a competition! Go to page 90 for instructions.

GRAMMAR FOCUS

Comparatives and superlatives of irregular adjectives

Adjective	Comparative	Superlative
good	better than	the best
bad	worse than	the worst
far	farther than	the farthest

As + adjective + as

Paris is **as beautiful as** Rome.

Remember! Use *as* + adjective + *as* to express equality.

7 Practice

Work with a partner. In your notebook, write sentences comparing the things listed below. Use the adjectives in parentheses.

1. reading/watching TV (*good*)

   Reading is better than watching TV.
2. headache/toothache (*bad*)
3. Saturn/Uranus/Pluto (*far from planet Earth*)
4. horror movie/action movie (*equally exciting*)

8 Practice

Read the quiz. Fill in the blanks with the correct form of the adjectives in parentheses. Then circle the correct answers.

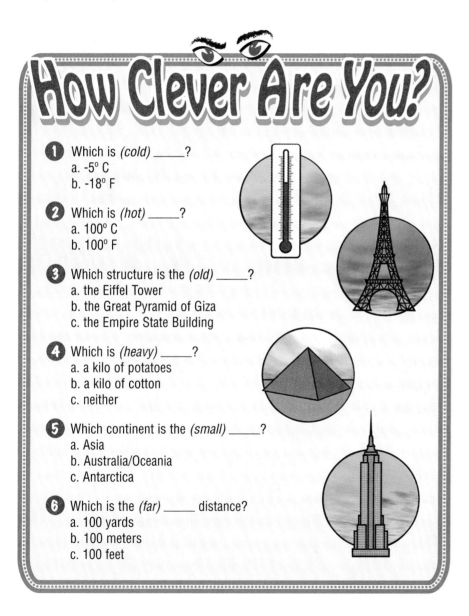

How Clever Are You?

1 Which is (*cold*) _____?
   a. -5° C
   b. -18° F

2 Which is (*hot*) _____?
   a. 100° C
   b. 100° F

3 Which structure is the (*old*) _____?
   a. the Eiffel Tower
   b. the Great Pyramid of Giza
   c. the Empire State Building

4 Which is (*heavy*) _____?
   a. a kilo of potatoes
   b. a kilo of cotton
   c. neither

5 Which continent is the (*small*) _____?
   a. Asia
   b. Australia/Oceania
   c. Antarctica

6 Which is the (*far*) _____ distance?
   a. 100 yards
   b. 100 meters
   c. 100 feet

9 Pronunciation

Questions with *which*

🎧 **Listen. Then practice the questions with a partner.**

1. Which is more interesting, the *Harry Potter* book or the movie?
2. Which do you like better, math or science?
3. Which do you prefer, jogging or biking?

10 Communication

Expressing preferences

Work in groups of three. Ask what each other's preferences are. Use the phrases below.

A: Which do you like better, hotdogs or hamburgers?
B: I like hamburgers better. How about you?

> **hot dogs/hamburgers
> video games/outdoor games
> play sports/watch TV
> loud music/soft music**

A Colossus of Rhodes

The Seven Ancient Wonders of the World

The seven ancient wonders of the world were the most impressive monuments of their time. Here are three of them.

THE HANGING GARDENS OF BABYLON

King Nebuchadnezzar II built the gardens for his wife. In people's minds, the Hanging Gardens were the most magnificent gardens ever made. People imagined the gardens with all kinds of exotic animals as well as fruit-bearing trees and flowers hanging from the palace terraces. However, this garden may not have existed except in the minds of poets and historians!

THE STATUE OF ZEUS AT OLYMPIA

This statue of ivory and gold was the most magnificent one ever made. It was built for the Greek god Zeus. The base of the statue was about 20 feet wide and 3 feet high. The statue alone was as tall as a four-story building!

THE COLOSSUS OF RHODES IN GREECE

The English word *colossal*, meaning "enormous," comes from this ancient wonder. The Colossus was huge! It took 900 camels to transport the broken pieces to Syria when an earthquake destroyed it. The people of Rhodes built the statue to celebrate the country's unity.

B Hanging Gardens of Babylon

C Great Pyramid of Giza

D Statue of Zeus

E Lighthouse of Alexandria

F Mausoleum at Halicarnassus

G Temple of Artemis

11 Reading and Listening

A. Read the article. Write *True* or *False*.

False 1. The word *colossus* means "small."

_____ 2. King Nebuchadnezzar I built the Hanging Gardens.

_____ 3. The statue of Zeus was made of ivory and gold.

_____ 4. The Colossus of Rhodes was in Rome.

B. 🎧 Listen. Write the letters of the correct pictures.

_F_ 1. The burial place for King Maussollos.

_____ 2. This temple served as a marketplace.

_____ 3. It is found in Egypt.

_____ 4. It guided sailors into the city.

12 Your Turn

Work with two classmates. Do research on "The Forgotten Wonders of the World." Choose one and write about it.

Learn to Learn

Using the Internet as a learning resource

The Internet is a wonderful research tool. It is also easy to use. Remember, just like any schoolwork, you will need your teacher's and parents' guidance when you use the Internet.

Progress Check *Units 9 and 10*

Grammar

A. Fill in the blanks with the correct form of the verbs in parentheses. (2 points each)

1. He *(play)* _was playing_ soccer when he *(break)* _broke_ his leg.

2. She *(dance)* _____ when she *(see)* _____ her teacher.

3. While I *(write)* _____ to him, he *(call)* _____.

4. While we *(watch)* _____ a scary movie, we *(see)* _____ someone outside.

5. They *(have)* _____ fun when they *(hear)* _____ the sad news.

6. While he *(jog)* _____, he *(meet)* _____ a friend.

B. Fill in the blanks with the comparative or superlative form of the adjective in parentheses. (1 point each)

1. Julie's car is *(clean)* _cleaner_ than Matt's.

2. Winter in Utah is *(cold)* _____ than in Illinois.

3. Is April *(hot)* _____ than September in your country?

4. She's *(good)* _____ at math than at English.

5. This is *(delicious)* _____ meal I've ever had.

6. That's *(bad)* _____ coffee ever.

C. Complete the chart with the missing adjective forms. (1 point each)

1. _big_	bigger	_biggest_
2. _____	_____	best
3. far	_____	_____
4. _____	longer	_____
5. famous	_____	_____
6. fast	_____	_____
7. _____	_____	tallest
8. _____	heavier	_____

Vocabulary

D. Circle the six weather adjectives. (1 point each)

```
C  L  E  W  D  S
W  L  R  S  U  R
I  C  O  F  G  A
N  H  Y  U  K  I
D  A  W  E  D  N
Y  F  O  G  G  Y
S  U  N  N  Y  M
B  U  S  P  D  O
```

Communication

E. Work with a partner. Take turns asking and answering the questions. (3 points each)

1. Which do you like better: 'NSync or The Backstreet Boys?

2. On weekends, do you prefer going out with your friends or staying at home with your family? Why?

3. Which do you like better, watching TV or going to the movies? Why?

Wide Angle on the world

1 Reading

A. Read the article on the right. Then circle the word that has a similar meaning.

1. ideal
   a. ordinary   b. normal   c. (perfect)
2. ancient
   a. very old   b. useful   c. new
3. attractive
   a. ugly   b. beautiful   c. simple
4. slim
   a. thin   b. short   c. heavy

B. Identify the following:

Olmec Indians   1. They liked men with broad nostrils and thick lips.

_____ 2. They favored snow-white skin and red lips.

_____ 3. Women in this country wear long metal rings around their necks.

_____ 4. In this culture, small, thin lips are considered attractive.

2 Speaking

Work in groups of six. Make a survey of the differences in what boys and girls think are attractive. Then fill in the chart.

A: In your opinion, what is your ideal of beauty?
B: In my opinion, a beautiful girl or a handsome boy has . . .

Feature or Trait	What boys find attractive	What girls find attractive
Hair	Long hair	
Eyes		
Lips		
Body build		
Height		

3 Writing

In your notebook, write about the results of your survey.

In my group, boys think long hair, big, brown eyes, and

small, thin lips are attractive.

What Is Beauty?

Images of beauty are all around us: in movies, on television, in magazines, and on the Internet. However, the ideal of beauty changes through the centuries and varies from culture to culture.

Thousands of years ago, men liked healthy women who could have children. Women liked strong, healthy men who would be able to hunt for food and protect the family. Among the Olmec Indians, for example, women liked men with broad nostrils, thick lips, and full cheeks.

The ancient Egyptian's ideal of beauty is similar to the modern, Western ideal—a slim body, muscles, and broad shoulders for men; small waists, flat stomachs, and long, thick hair for women.

During the sixteenth century in England, the ideal woman had snow-white skin and red cheeks and lips. Women during those days applied very white makeup to their faces and their necks. But Elizabethan women did not take baths very often!

In Burma, a beautiful woman is one with a very long neck. Girls from the age of five or six wear metal rings around their necks to make them longer. As the neck grows longer, more rings are added.

In Asian cultures, small, thin lips are considered attractive, but in Western cultures, large, full lips are preferred. Some movie stars and models even have cosmetic surgery to make their lips larger!

But is physical beauty that important? Think about it.

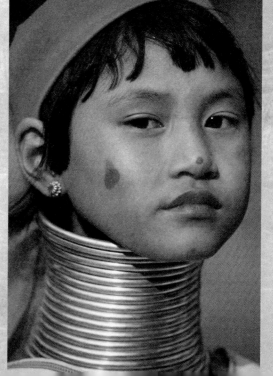

11 You should get some rest.

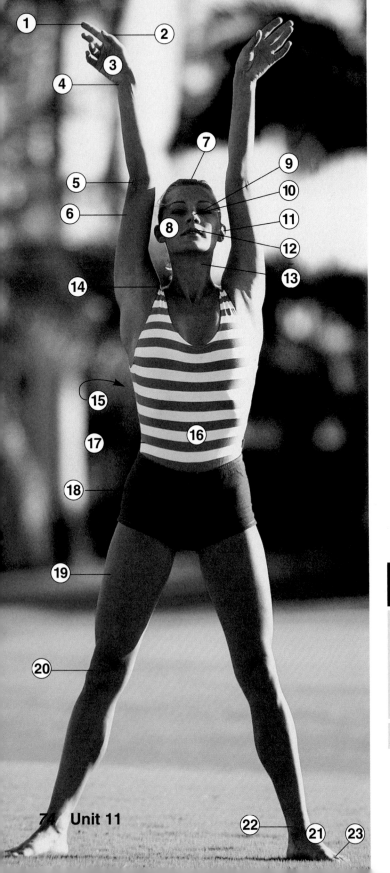

Learning Goals

Communication
Give advice

Grammar
Should/Shouldn't
Habitual past: *used to*

Vocabulary
Parts of the body
Common illnesses

1 Vocabulary

A. 🎧 Listen and repeat. Then match the numbers on the photo with the parts of the body listed below.

_6_ arm	__ finger	__ mouth	__ stomach
__ foot *(feet)*	__ thumb	__ hand	__ face
__ neck	__ hip	__ toe	__ waist
__ head	__ eye	__ shoulder	__ leg
__ ear	__ wrist	__ elbow	__ nose
__ back	__ knee	__ ankle	

B. Write the words from Exercise A in the correct column.

Head	Body	Arm	Leg
eye	_____	_____	_____
_____	_____	_____	_____
_____	_____	_____	_____
_____	_____	_____	_____
_____	_____	_____	_____
_____	_____	_____	_____

GRAMMAR FOCUS

Should/Shouldn't

Affirmative statements	**Negative statements**
You **should see** a doctor.	He **should not do** that.
They **should get** some rest.	They **shouldn't work** so hard.

Remember! Use *should* to give advice.

2 Practice

Read the situations below. Write your advice, using *should* and the expressions in the box.

go to bed	call her	study tonight
tell his parents		take some aspirin

1. I have a fever and a headache.
   You should take some aspirin.

2. Janet is tired and sleepy.
   _____

3. The students have a test tomorrow.
   _____

4. Daniel broke an expensive vase.
   _____

5. I miss my sister in the United States.
   _____

3 Practice

What shouldn't the people in the pictures below do? Write sentences in your notebook.

1. She shouldn't litter.

1. litter

2. sleep all day

3. watch too much TV

4. eat too much ice cream

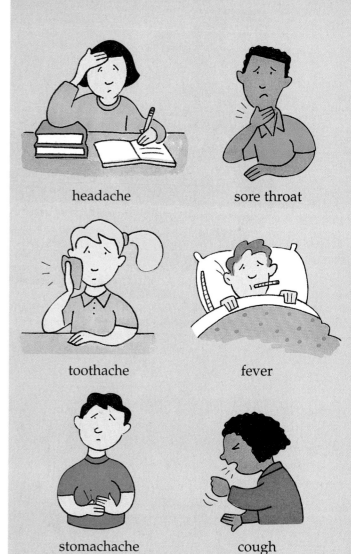

headache   sore throat

toothache   fever

stomachache   cough

4 Communication

Asking for and giving advice on common illnesses

A. ⌒ Listen and repeat.

A: What's the matter?
B: I have a headache.
A: I'm sorry to hear that. You should take some aspirin.

B. Work with a partner. Choose one of the pictures above. Use *should* and one of the phrases below to role-play a situation. Use the dialogue in Exercise A as a model.

see a doctor	rest	take aspirin
take some medicine		see a dentist

5 Dialogue

🎧 **Listen and read. Underline Paul's reason for choosing Alex over Lori.**

Paul: Hi, Lori. I have something for you. It's the script for the spring show.

Lori: Thanks, Paul. I'll read it tonight.

Paul: What's the matter? A new script used to make you happy.

Lori: I have a headache.

Paul: You should go home and rest then. Maybe take some aspirin.

Lori: Paul, can I ask you something?

Paul: Sure.

Lori: Why did you choose Alex for the summer program in Michigan? Why didn't you give me a chance?

Paul: I'm sorry, Lori, but Alex was the best candidate for it. The program director asked for a male performer.

Lori: Is that the reason? I feel ridiculous. I'm sorry, Paul.

Paul: I understand how you feel, Lori. I used to get upset about these kinds of things, too.

Lori: Thanks for understanding, Paul.

6 Comprehension

Correct the wrong information.

headache
1. Lori has a ~~fever~~.
2. Paul did not have a good reason for recommending Alex.
3. Paul thinks Lori was the best candidate for the summer program.
4. Lori knew the reason for Paul's decision.

GRAMMAR FOCUS

Habitual past: *used to*

Affirmative statement
I **used to drink** a lot of soda. I don't anymore.

Negative statement
I **didn't use to drink** milk. Now, I do.

Yes/No **questions**
Did you **use to drink** milk?

Answers
Yes, I **did**. / No, I **didn't**.

Remember! *Used to* expresses past habits or situations that no longer exist in the present.

7 Practice

A. Look at the picture of the class reunion. Then read the sentences describing the people in the picture.

1. Shelley is now heavy and unattractive.
2. Kristi is very fashionable.
3. Ken is heavy.
4. Matt is now a handsome movie star.
5. Pam is now very attractive.

B. Now look at their high-school picture. In your notebook, write two sentences for each describing what they used to look like at the time.

1. *Shelley:* thin and beautiful / very popular
   Shelley used to be thin and beautiful.
   She used to be very popular.
2. *Kristi:* shy and unattractive / long hair
3. *Ken:* not heavy / handsome
4. *Matt:* chubby / bookworm
5. *Pam:* very curly hair / not beautiful

8 Listening

🎧 **Work with a partner. Listen twice to the conversation. Then answer the *Yes/No* questions.**

Yes, she did. 1. Did Karen's mom use to walk to school?

_____ 2. Did the family use to go to the movies?

_____ 3. Was life easy during the Depression?

_____ 4. Did Karen's grandfather use to sing for entertainment?

9 Your Turn

A. What did you use to do as a child that you don't do now? Write a paragraph in your notebook. Share it with the class.

When I was a child, I used to cry every time Mom went to work. Now I like it when my parents are away.

B. Work with a partner. Ask *Yes/No* questions about each other's lives when you were children.

CLASS REUNION 2005

HIGH SCHOOL PROM 1985

Unit 11   77

10 Reading

Personology Test

A. Find out what your face is trying to tell you. Look at the picture and read the descriptions.

11 Speaking

Sit face-to-face with a classmate. Try to give him or her one piece of advice based on a facial feature. Remember: This is all for fun!

A: Hmm. Your ears lay flat. You should be careful with your money.

B: Really?

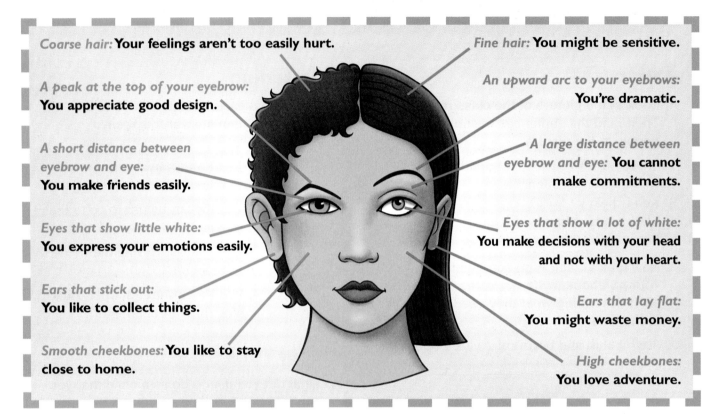

Coarse hair: **Your feelings aren't too easily hurt.**

A peak at the top of your eyebrow: **You appreciate good design.**

A short distance between eyebrow and eye: **You make friends easily.**

Eyes that show little white: **You express your emotions easily.**

Ears that stick out: **You like to collect things.**

Smooth cheekbones: **You like to stay close to home.**

Fine hair: **You might be sensitive.**

An upward arc to your eyebrows: **You're dramatic.**

A large distance between eyebrow and eye: **You cannot make commitments.**

Eyes that show a lot of white: **You make decisions with your head and not with your heart.**

Ears that lay flat: **You might waste money.**

High cheekbones: **You love adventure.**

B. Match the adjective with the physical feature. You may use a dictionary.

__E__ 1. an upward arc to the eyebrows   A. sensitive

____ 2. ears that stick out   B. friendly

____ 3. high cheekbones   C. emotional

____ 4. short distance between eyebrow and eye   D. adventurous

____ 5. fine hair   E. dramatic

____ 6. eyes that show little white   F. like to collect things

12 Writing

Choose a favorite picture of yourself when you were a child and one now that you're a teenager. Write a paragraph about these pictures.

I was three years old in this picture. I used to have curly hair. My legs were short and fat. I used to fall every time I ran to my mother. This is me now. My hair is short. I am tall and thin. People say I could be a fashion model.

Joe's Advice to Lori

🎧 Listen and read. Then answer these questions orally:

What should Lori say to Alex? What should Alex say to Lori?

12 Will you call us?

1 Dialogue

🎧 **Listen and read. How long is the summer program?**

Joe: Come on, Alex. Did you pass the audition?

Alex: Well . . .

Diane: Well what, Alex? Did you or did you not?

Alex: I did it! I'm in!

All: Really? Congratulations!

Joe: Boy, we'll really miss you. It won't be the same around here without you.

Diane: You should e-mail us, Alex. And will you call us, too?

Alex: Very funny.

Lori: Umm. Alex, can I talk to you?

Alex: Sure, Lori. What is it?

Lori: I want to apologize. I'm really sorry about my reaction. As a friend, I should have been happy for you.

Alex: It's OK, Lori. Your reaction was normal.

Lori: And will you write to me?

Alex: Of course I will, Lori. Come on, guys. The program is only for six weeks!

2 Comprehension

Answer these questions:

1. Who will go to Michigan?
2. What two things does Diane ask Alex to do?
3. Who feels bad about not being a good friend?

GRAMMAR FOCUS

Future tense: *will*

Affirmative statements	**Negative statements**
I **will write** you everyday.	I **will not forget** you.
We **will go** skating this weekend.	We **will not go** out this weekend.
***Yes/No* Questions**	**Short answers**
Will they **come** to the game?	Yes, they **will**.
Will he **be** there?	No, he **won't**.

Remember! **Contractions** I will = **I'll** it will = **it'll** will not = **won't**

3 Pronunciation

The sound /// in contractions

A. 🎧 **Listen and repeat.**

I'll   she'll   he'll   it'll   you'll   we'll   they'll

B. 🎧 **Listen and repeat.**

1. I'll meet you tomorrow at two.
2. They'll arrive in the evening.
3. We'll leave at three.

4 Practice

A. Read the ad for a summer program in China.

Be a Student Ambassador to China This Summer

Here are four reasons to join.

1. Live with a Chinese family.

2. Make new friends.

3. Learn a new language quickly.

4. Experience a new culture.

What the program will cover:

- Cost of air travel to and from China
- Cost of living with a host family
- Tuition for summer classes in China

What the program will not cover:

- Spending money or allowance
- Costs for visa application
- Personal tours

B. In your notebook, write three sentences stating what will happen when you join the summer program to China.

I'll live with a Chinese family.

C. Work with a partner. Write five *Yes/No* questions in your notebook to find out what the program will and will not cover.

Will the program cover the cost of air travel?

5 Vocabulary

Summer activities

Label the pictures of summer activities using the words below.

> travel/go abroad
> attend summer camp
> take summer classes
> train in athletics
> find a job
> volunteer

1. *train in athletics*

2. _____

3. _____

4. _____

5. _____

6. _____

6 Your Turn

With a partner, talk about your summer plans. In the chart below, write what you *will* and *won't* do this summer.

Things I'll do this summer:
Things I won't do this summer:

GRAMMAR FOCUS

May and might

I **may (not) go** abroad this summer.
They **might (not) travel** this summer.

> **Remember!** *May* and *might* express possibility.
> *Will* expresses something that is sure to happen.
> I **may/might** be late tomorrow. *(It's possible I'll be late tomorrow.)*
> I **will** be late tomorrow. *(I'm sure I will be late.)*

7 Practice

Fill in the blanks with the correct answer.

Dan: Remember, we're studying together for our finals tonight.

Jim: Don't worry. I *(1. will, may)* __will__ be there.

Dan: Where's Eric? *(2. Will, May)* _____ he join us?

Jim: He went home sick. He definitely *(3. may not, won't)* _____ be coming.

Dan: Hey, look! That woman looks sick.

Jim: Oh yeah. Let's go check. She *(4. will, may)* _____ need help.

Dan: Whew. Thank God, she's all right. So are we going to the movies on Saturday?

Jim: Definitely! I *(5. will, may)* _____ call you Friday night to make plans.

8 Practice

Write a paragraph about what you will definitely and probably *(might)* do on Saturday.

My Plans for Saturday:

I might get up late on Saturday. I'll clean my room. After that I'll...

9 Communication

Expressing possibilities

A. ⌒ Listen and repeat.

A: What will you do this summer?
B: I'm not sure. I might take karate lessons.

B. Work with a partner. Use your charts from Exercise 6 to talk about what you will do this summer.

10 Information Gap

Student A, go to page 91. Student B, go to page 92. Follow the instructions.

11 Reading

Read the article about volunteering.

Why volunteer?

During the summer, how many times do you say, "Mom, I'm bored!"? For many teenagers, summer is a time to relax and vacation. But in many parts of the world, a lot of teenagers spend their summers volunteering.

There are a lot of volunteering opportunities right in your community. Below are examples:

Homeless shelters: In these shelters, you might help prepare and serve meals, work in the shelter's office and help collect food and clothes.

Food banks: You might help collect and distribute food to those in need.

Special Olympics: This is an international organization that offers sports programs for people with disabilities. You might want to help with sports training, fund raising, competition planning, and office work.

Parks: Many parks need help maintaining the area and educating the public on preservation.

Habitat for Humanity: This organization builds and gives houses to poor people. As a volunteer, you will not only help others, but you will also learn about building houses.

Hospitals, nursing homes, libraries, animal shelters, the Red Cross, your local church: These places need volunteers all the time.

12 Comprehension

Match the organizations in column A with the descriptions in column B.

A	B
_d_ 1. Habitat for Humanity	a. Collect and distribute food.
____ 2. Special Olympics	b. Educate people on maintaining public parks.
____ 3. parks	c. Provide temporary homes to the homeless.
____ 4. food banks	d. Build houses for the poor.
____ 5. homeless shelters	e. Plan activities for the disabled.

13 Speaking

Work in groups of three. Discuss these questions:

1. Why should teenagers like you volunteer?
2. Where can you volunteer in your community? Mention two places.
3. List what you can do for one of these places.

14 Writing

Work with a partner. List some organizations in your community where teenagers can volunteer. Post your list on the class bulletin board.

Progress Check *Units 11 and 12*

Grammar

A. Unscramble the sentences to make questions. Then write short answers using the cues in parentheses. (2 points each)

1. Jose/German/next year/will/study/?
   Will Jose study German next year?

   (No/English) *No, he won't. He'll study English.*

2. she/to/France/will/go/?/this summer
   _____

   (Yes) _____

3. bring/a cake/they/will/to the party/?
   _____

   (No/apple pie) _____

4. will/to/the/dance/we/go/this weekend/?
   _____

   (No/rock concert) _____

5. be nice/the weather/will/this weekend/?
   _____

   (Yes) _____

B. Write sentences describing what the people used to do and what they do now. Follow the example. (2 points each)

1. *before:* Pablo/live/Spain; *now:* in Venezuela
   Pablo used to live in Spain, but now he lives

   in Venezuela.

2. *before:* Maria/study/jazz dancing; *now:* ballet
   _____

3. *before:* I/like/Britney Spears; *now:* Christina Aguilera
   _____

4. *before:* He/drink coffee with milk; *now:* black coffee
   _____

Vocabulary

C. Circle the eight illnesses. (1 point each)

S	T	O	M	A	C	H	A	C	H	E
B	O	R	N	S	H	E	A	D	F	G
C	T	O	O	T	H	A	C	H	E	A
C	F	J	M	O	P	D	S	U	K	L
O	M	E	E	H	C	A	R	A	E	T
U	C	A	V	Z	Y	C	O	G	H	S
G	S	O	R	E	T	H	R	O	A	T
H	E	A	C	H	R	E	N	J	K	O
C	H	I	L	L	S	G	A	H	E	Z

D. Match a verb from the first column with a noun or phrase from the second column. Write the letter on the line. (1 point each)

_c_ 1. attend   a. in athletics

____ 2. go   b. a job

____ 3. take   c. summer camp

____ 4. learn   d. summer classes

____ 5. find   e. a new skill

____ 6. train   f. abroad

Communication

E. Work with a partner. Take turns reading the problems below and offering advice. Use should and shouldn't in your advice. (3 points each)

1. I don't feel well. I have a headache.
2. I don't understand the lesson.
3. I'm thirsty.
4. I'm tired.

F. Work with a partner. Tell your partner three things you might/may do after classes today. (3 points each)

SONG

Backstreet Boys

Backstreet Boys Kevin Richardson, Nicholas Carter, Brian Littrell, Alexander McLean, and Howie Dorough have everything teenagers love: great songs, good looks, and terrific dance moves. The band's first success in the United States was the single "Everybody," which was a major hit in 1998. Their first album, "Backstreet Boys," sold over 10 million copies.

The One

I'll be the one
I guess you were lost when I met you
Still there were tears in your eyes
So out of trust and I knew
No more than mysteries and lies

There you were, wild and free
Reachin' out like you needed me
A helping hand to make it right
I am holding you all through the night

Chorus

I'll be the one
Who will make all your sorrows undone
I'll be the light
When you feel like there's nowhere to run
I'll be the one to hold you
And make sure that you'll be alright

'Cause my faith is gone
And I want to take you from darkness to light
There you were, wild and free
Reachin' out like you needed me
A helping hand to make it right
I am holding you all through the night

Repeat chorus

You need me like I need you
We can share our dreams comin' true
I can show you what true love means
Just take my hand, baby, please

I'll be the one, I'll be the light
Where you can run to make it alright
I'll be the one, I'll be the light
Where you can run

Repeat chorus

1. ∩ Work with a partner. Read the lyrics and find words in the song that rhyme with the words below. Then listen to the song.
   • you • eyes • free • right • one

2. List all the people in your life who could be:
   • *a helping hand*
   • *a light you can turn to when you feel like there's nowhere to run*

   Discuss your list with a partner.

GAME Say and Do the Opposite

Steps

1. Look at the pictures of the girl and learn the new words.

2. Divide into two teams. A person from one team stands and challenges a person from the other team, who also stands. The challenger rubs, points at, touches, or pats a part of his body, but says he is doing something different. The person from the other team must *do* and *say* the opposite. For example, if the challenger rubs his stomach and says, "I am patting my head," the other player must pat her head and say "I am rubbing my stomach."

3. The challenger gets three tries to get the other player to make a mistake. If the other player makes a mistake, the challenger's team gets one point. If not, the other team gets one point.

4. Teams switch roles and challengers after each play. Your teacher will keep score on the board.

rub

point at

touch

pat

Fun with Grammar

Unit 1, 3 Practice, page 5

For the teacher:

1. Before playing, decide on five categories for the game. Possible categories include: *classmates, Hollywood actors, international bands, famous local singers, 6th grade teachers at our school.*
2. Have students play Ten Questions. Divide the class into two teams. Announce the category for this round of the game. For example, the category for the first round is "classmates."
3. Write the name of one student from the class on an index card.
4. The first student from Team 1 (T1) comes to the front of the room and looks at the name on the card. Students from Team 2 (T2) can ask ten questions. The Team 1 student can answer only with *yes* or *no* answers.

   For example:

   T2: Is the person a girl?   T2: Is she tall?
   T1: Yes, she is.   T1: No, she isn't.

5. After ten questions (or sooner), Team 2 tries to guess the classmate's name. If they guess correctly, they get 300 points. If they are wrong, Team 1 has a chance to try to guess. If they guess correctly, they get 200 points. If they are wrong, then Team 2 gets a final chance. If Team 2 guesses correctly this time, they get 100 points.
6. The game continues in this manner until all the cards have been used.

Unit 6, 8 Practice, page 40

For the teacher:

1. Distribute slips of paper to each student. The paper slips should be big enough to accommodate a sentence or two.
2. Tell the students to write a prediction. The prediction can be funny, serious, or silly. Remind students to use the future tense of *be going to* + verb. For example, *You're going to travel soon.* Write some common phrases used in predictions on the board for students who don't have the needed vocabulary.
3. Collect the predictions and put them in a box.
4. Have students randomly pick a prediction from the box.
5. Invite students to read the predictions aloud.
6. You might want to write some of the predictions on the board and have the class check if the correct verb forms are used.

Unit 7, 5 Practice, page 48

For the teacher:

1. Write the following verbs on the board:

open	clap	wash
stop	smile	drop
carry	worry	enjoy
enjoy	plan	cry

2. Have students write the simple past form of each verb in their notebooks. Give them one minute to do this.
3. After one minute, tell students to stop writing.
4. Have students exchange work to correct the answers.
5. The student who got the most number of correct answers wins.

Unit 8, 2 Practice, page 52

For the teacher:

1. Divide the class into two teams.
2. Cut a piece of paper into eight squares.
3. Write one adjective on each piece of paper and put them in a box or container.
4. Invite a student from the first team to draw an adjective from the box. The student must act out the adjective for his or her teammates. Set a time limit.
5. If the team does not guess the adjective, the other team has a chance to answer and "steal" the point.
6. You might want to include other adjectives previously learned in this book.

Unit 8, 4 Practice, page 53

For the teacher:

1. Divide the class into two teams. Give list A to Team A; list B to Team B. Tell them to memorize the past forms of the verbs. After three minutes, take the lists away.
2. On the board, make two lists of the base forms of some of the verbs. Each list should have the same lists arranged in different order.
3. Have a representative from each team go to the board and choose any verb to write in the past form.
4. Each student should write only one verb, but he or she may correct the previous student's answer. The first team to give all correct answers wins.

List A	List B
break	has
bring	go
do	teach
drive	do
get	tell
go	break
has	stand
sleep	take
stand	get
take	drive
teach	bring
tell	sleep

Fun with Grammar

Unit 8, 6 Practice, page 53

For the teacher:

1. Create groups of five and assign a number to each student in the group. Have each group sit in a circle.
2. Student 1 starts by saying what he or she did last Saturday.
3. Student 2 tells the group what Student 1 did and adds what he/she, Student 2, did.
4. Then it's Student 3's turn to do as Student 2 did in Step 3.
5. Continue with this pattern until every person in the group has added a sentence.

Unit 9, 6 Practice, page 61

For the teacher:

1. Choose two or three volunteers from the class. These students will pantomime sentences.
2. Divide the rest of the class into two teams.
3. Choose sentences from Exercises 4 and 5 on page 61. Whisper a sentence to the volunteers and explain the actions to them. The volunteers act out the sentence.
4. The teams try to guess the sentence based on the actions.
5. The team that first guesses the sentence correctly gets the point.

Unit 10, 6 Practice, page 68

For the teacher:

1. Prepare a list of adjectives and nouns for students to match. Below are suggestions.

big	difficult
fast	interesting
expensive	

Asia	airplane
Africa	Chinese (language)
Harry Potter books	the Concorde
Toyota	*The History of Mathematics*
Europe	Rolls Royce
French (language)	Mercedes Benz

2. Divide the class into two teams.
3. Have each team choose three adjectives and the nouns that can go with their adjectives.
4. Each team writes sentences comparing the nouns they have chosen.
   For example, *Chinese is more difficult than French.* Set a time limit (10 minutes).
5. Have a representative from each team read out the sentences while you write them on the board.
6. Have the class correct any errors in the sentences. The team with the highest number of correct sentences wins.

Information Gaps

Unit 5, 6 Information Gap, page 35

Look at your picture. Ask and answer questions about the activities in your picture.

A: Is the Dad reading a newspaper in your picture?
B: No, he's not.
A: What's he doing?
B: He's watching TV. My turn.

Unit 12, 10 Information Gap, page 83

The chart below lists the summer plans of a group of friends. Take turns asking and answering questions. Put a check (✔) next to the activity each person is going to do.

A: What will Martha do this summer?
B: She might take swimming lessons. What will John do this summer?

Summer activities	Martha	John	Tony	Bob	Gina	Jane
take swimming lessons						
travel abroad		✔				
take dance lessons				✔		
go to summer camp						
get a babysitting job						
hang out at home					✔	

Information Gaps

Unit 5, 6 Information Gap, page 35

Look at your picture. Ask and answer questions about the activities in your picture.

B: Is the Mom reading a book to Austin in your picture?
A: No, she's not.
B: What's she doing?
A: She's working on the computer. My turn.

Unit 12, 10 Information Gap, page 83

The chart below lists the summer plans of a group of friends. Take turns asking and answering questions. Put a check (✔) next to the activity each person is going to do.

B: What will John do this summer?
A: He might . . .

Summer activities	Martha	John	Tony	Bob	Gina	Jane
take swimming lessons	✔					
travel abroad						
take dance lessons						
go to summer camp			✔			
get a babysitting job						✔
hang out at home						

Project 1 A Snapshot of a Great Snack

Think of a great snack that you can make. Write instructions on how to make it. Use the recipe below as a guide. Then pretend you're on a cooking show. Explain and demonstrate how to make the snack to your group or class.

A. Write the ingredients you need.

To make a Chicago hot dog, you need a hot dog, a hot dog bun, an onion, a tomato, a hot pepper, and a dill pickle. You also need some mustard, relish, and celery salt.

B. Write the steps in the recipe.

First, boil the hot dog for about three minutes, until it's nice and fat.

Next, chop the onion and slice the tomato. Then slice the hot pepper and pickle.

When the hot dog is ready, put it in the bun. Then add the other ingredients in this order: First, put some mustard on the hot dog. I like to use a lot of mustard. Then put some relish on. After that, put about a teaspoon of chopped onion on top.

Finally, add a slice of pickle, three slices of tomato, the hot pepper, and sprinkle the whole thing with celery salt. Mmm, it tastes good!

Project 2 A Snapshot of Your Hobby

Choose one of your hobbies or free-time activities to write about. Use the project below as a guide. Share information about your hobby with your partner, group, or class.

A. Write about your hobby, how often you do it, and why you like it.

I'm really into snorkeling. My family goes to Key West, Florida every year. I go snorkeling almost every day when we're there. Snorkeling is really fun. It's a totally different world underwater. You can see lots of cool tropical fish and coral. And you can learn to hold your breath for a long time.

B. Write about how you got started with your hobby.

I went snorkeling for the first time when I was seven. My cousin Richard taught me how. He's five years older than I. First, we practiced in a swimming pool. Then we did it at the beach. Finally, my uncle took us out on his boat to an awesome coral reef, and — wow! I fell in love with snorkeling after that.

C. Write about what you have done.

Last summer, my cousin and I took a weekend trip to Fort Jefferson in Key West. Fort Jefferson is an old fort on an island. You can camp there for three dollars. The water was super clear, and I saw lots of neat fish. I also saw some beautiful barracuda.

D. Write about future plans.

Next summer, I'm going to learn how to scuba dive. I mow my neighbors' lawns to earn some money, and I'm saving my earnings. Someday, I'm going to go diving all over the world. I'll go to the Great Barrier Reef in Australia, the Maldives in the Indian Ocean, and the Galapagos Islands of Ecuador. But first, I have to save enough money for the scuba-diving lessons. That means many summers of doing more yard work for my neighbors.

Project 3 A Snapshot of My Childhood

Write about your life when you were five or six years old. Choose from the list of topics on the right. Use the project below as a guide. Share your project with a classmate and see how many things you have in common.

Music
TV shows
Toys and games
Books and magazines
Pets
Foods
Collections
Things you loved
Things you hated
Your family
Your neighborhood
Favorite places
Dreams

A. Choose four topics to write about.

B. Find pictures from your childhood to include with your writing.

My Dreams
When I was five, I wanted to be a famous sports star. I used to want to be a famous football player or a famous hockey player. Hey, I'm not famous, but I'm on the football team this year!

My Neighborhood
When I was five, I lived in Seattle, Washington. I remember it used to rain a lot. There was a creek near my house. My friends and I used to hang out there and explore.

My Favorite Toys and Games
I used to play Nintendo a lot. I was really into Mario Brothers and Duck Hunt. My brother and I had a big Hot Wheels collection. We used to race them around the house and make them crash. We also used to play with Ninja Turtles and Power Rangers action figures. You can guess what my favorite TV shows were.

My Favorite Foods
My mom and dad used to work long hours, so my brother and I used to eat a lot of fast foods. Macaroni and cheese was my favorite, along with pizza and hot dogs. I used to hate peas, by the way.

Games from Around

In many countries, children and teenagers love to play games. Here are games from different parts of the world.

❶ "Marco Polo" from the United States

This game is played in a swimming pool. One person closes his or her eyes and counts to ten. The other people swim to other parts of the pool. With eyes still closed, the person tries to find the other people. He or she calls out "Marco," and the others have to say "Polo." The game ends when someone is caught. That person has to find the others in the next game.

❷ "Take from the End" from Japan

This game is played in pairs or groups. One person says a word that does not end with the "n" sound, for example, "baseball." The next person says a word that begins with the last sound in that word, for example, "love." The next person says a word beginning with the last sound in that word, for example, "very." If someone says a word ending with an "n" sound, the team loses.

❸ "The Hunter" from Saudi Arabia

One person is "the hunter." The hunter closes his or her eyes, while the other people run and hide. Then the hunter starts looking for them. When the hunter finds someone, the person starts running and the hunter has to catch that person. The game finally ends when the hunter catches everyone. The first person caught is the next hunter.

❹ "Caught You!" from China

A group of people sits in a circle. One person sits outside the circle, with his or her back to the group, eyes closed. The group quietly passes a small ball from person to person. The person outside the circle says "Stop!" The person caught holding the ball has to stand up and sing a song or tell a story.

the World

1 Comprehension

Read the descriptions of the games on page 96. Then complete each sentence with the correct game.

1. ___Marco Polo___ is played in water.
2. _____ uses a ball.
3. _____ is similar to the game Hide-and-Seek.
4. _____ is a word game.
5. In _____ , someone catches another person.
6. In _____ , someone has to sing or tell a story.

2 Discussion

Work with a partner. Discuss the questions.

1. Which two games are the most similar?
2. Are any of these games similar to games played in your country? If so, which ones?
3. What are some other games people play in your country?

3 Playing

Play "Take from the End" (in English) or "Caught you." If you get caught with the ball, you have to stand up and sing a song in English or say four funny sentences about yourself, for example, "I like to eat shoes."

4 Writing

Work with a small group. Choose a game people play in your country. Discuss the rules and then write a description of the game in your notebook.

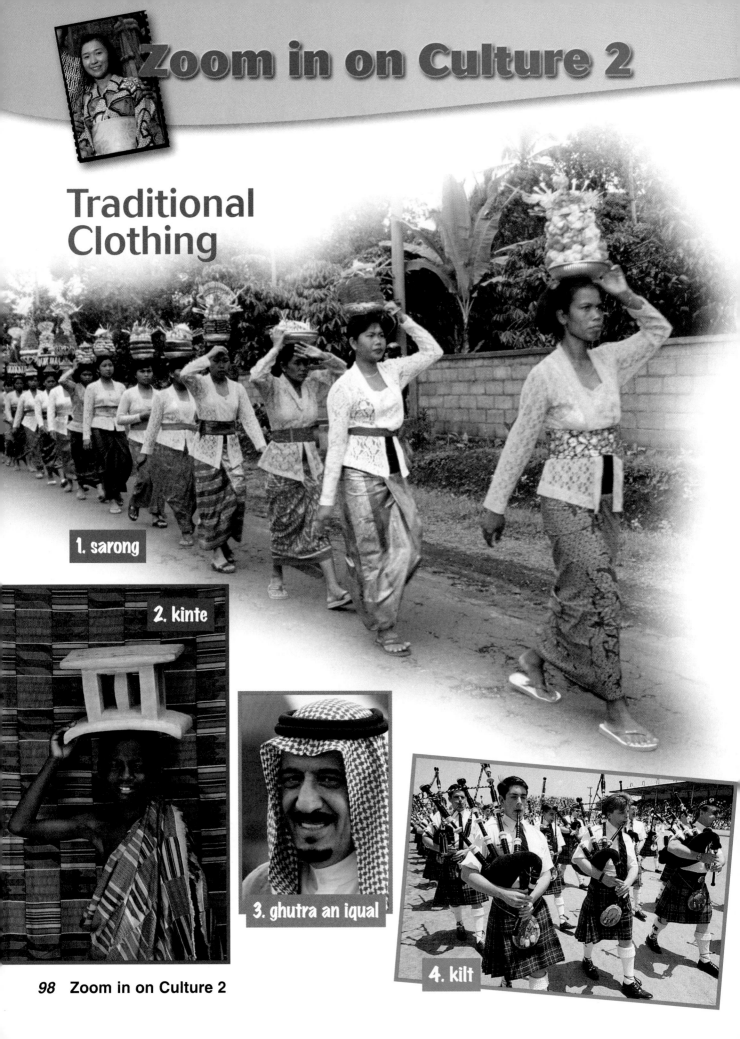

Traditional Clothing

1. sarong

2. kinte

3. ghutra an iqual

4. kilt

1 Comprehension

A. Look at the pictures on page 98. Read the descriptions of traditional clothing below and fill in the name of the clothing item.

1. Men in this northern country sometimes wear a ____kilt____ on special occasions. It is a short wool skirt, usually plaid. It is held up with a wide black belt. Men say these are warm and comfortable.

2. Men and women in this tropical country usually wear a _____ because this clothing is cool and comfortable. It is a piece of cotton cloth that is tied around the waist. It usually comes in beautiful prints, but it also comes in solid colors. People usually wear modern shirts or blouses with these.

3. Men wear _____ all year round in this country. This headdress is made of cotton and is either white or red-and-white check. It is held on the head with a black cord.

4. Men and women in this country sometimes wear _____ on special occasions. It is a beautiful multi-colored piece of cloth. It can be worn over the shoulders. Women also tie it under the arms to make a dress.

5. In the summer, men and women in this country sometimes wear _____ to festivals. It is a light cotton robe, held closed with a wide sash. Women's robes are usually in colorful prints, while men's robes are usually blue and white.

B. Look at the pictures again. Point to the following in the pictures:

1. check
2. plaid
3. cord
4. sash
5. multi-colored
6. print

C. Write the number of the clothing item next to the country where you think it is worn.

__4__ Scotland _____ Saudi Arabia _____ Japan

_____ Ghana _____ Indonesia

5. yukata

2 Discussion

Work with a partner. Discuss these questions.

1. Which of the traditional clothing items would you like to wear?
2. Which of the clothing items would you not like to wear? Why?
3. What are some traditional clothing items in your country or region?

3 Writing

Work with a small group. Find a picture of traditional clothing used in a region in your country. In your notebook, write a description of this clothing.

Travel Destination

Bali: A Magical Island

Asia has some of the most beautiful countries and the most interesting cultures in the world. One of the most beautiful places in Asia is Bali in Indonesia. Bali is a little smaller than Trinidad, with a population about the same size as Costa Rica's. The Balinese speak Bahasa Bali and Indonesian. In tourist areas, many can speak English.

Bali is famous for its beautiful green jungles, terraced rice fields, and many temples.

No visitor to Bali should miss its dances and music. The most famous Balinese dance is the "Legong," an ancient palace dance. Only young girls ages five to fourteen can perform the Legong. The dancers wear heavy make-up, beautiful golden costumes, and crowns decorated with flowers. They twist and turn to Balinese music played by a gamelon orchestra. *Gamelon* means to hammer, and the special sound of Balinese music comes from the "hammering" of xylophones and gongs.

Bali is also famous for its colorful and unique festivals. There are festivals every day on the island—you may even see two or three. The biggest festival is *Nyepi*, the Balinese New Year. The day before Nyepi is the noisiest day of the year. People hit pots and pans together, shoot fireworks, and play music. Nyepi itself is the quietest and the darkest day of the year. No people or cars can be on the streets, and no lights or electricity can be used at home. The Balinese believe the New Year should begin in darkness and silence.

1

2

1 Comprehension

A. Read the article about Bali. Then match the Balinese word with its definition.

_____ 1. Bahasa Bali   a. Balinese orchestra

_____ 2. Nyepi   b. Balinese dance

_____ 3. Legong   c. Balinese language

_____ 4. Gamelon   d. Balinese New Year

B. Read the descriptions and look at the pictures. Write the number of the correct picture next to each description.

_____ festival   _____ terraced rice fields

_____ Legong dance   _____ gamelon orchestra

2 Discussion

Work with a partner. Discuss these questions:

1. Imagine you can go to Bali. What one thing do you most want to see or do?
2. What are some things in Bali that are similar to your country?
3. What are some things in Bali that are different from your country?

3 Writing

Work in small groups. Write an advertisement to attract tourists to your country, using the topics below as your guide. Use adjectives, comparatives, and superlatives. Bring in a picture for the ad, if possible.

- a general description of your country
- a description of the capital city
- a description of activities in a tourist city
- other activities people can do in your country
- a special kind of dance in your country
- a special kind of music in your country
- a famous festival in your country

Useful Words and Expressions

UNIT 1

Nouns
best friend
director
drama group
football player
guitar
musician

Adjectives
athletic
favorite
friendly
funny
good-looking
great
handsome
heavy
old
pretty
serious
smart
strong
tall
thin

Verbs
be (*am, is, are*)
hang out
has/have
live
want

Expressions
Guess what?
How about you?
Let me guess.
Let's go!
Nothing much.
What does he/she look like?
What's up?
Whose book is that?

UNIT 2

Nouns
chocolate chips
cookies
dough
flour
ginger ale
ingredients
olive(s)
pepperoni

pineapple
pizza
recipe
refrigerator
restaurant
tablespoon
teaspoon
tomato sauce
vinegar
yeast

Verbs
bake
blend
burn
chop
crack
drizzle
flatten
melt
pour
sprinkle
stir

Expressions
chat on the Internet
do homework
get together with friends
have a snack
listen to music
play video games
spend time with family
talk on the phone
watch TV
Let's go for it!
What do we need?

UNIT 3

Nouns
candy
cereal
fish
ice cream
soda

Expressions of quantity
a bag of onions / a bag of chips
a box of strawberries / a box of
  cookies
a bunch of carrots
a dozen eggs
a gallon of milk / a gallon of ice
  cream

a half pound of cheese
a head of lettuce
a loaf of bread
a pound of ham
a quart of orange juice

Expressions
We're just hanging out.
Come on.
I think we're in a lot of trouble.
What else?
Let's get together soon!

UNIT 4

Nouns
bowling
dancing
free time
hobby
ice skating
in-line skating
skating rink
surfing

Verbs
enjoy + gerund
go + gerund
hate + gerund
like + gerund
love + gerund
need
plan

Adverbs
once a year
twice a month
three times a week
every day
never

Expressions
He's a couch potato.
How often do you play
  basketball?
Is reading your only hobby?
Not really.
Nothing much.
What do you enjoy doing?
What do you like to do?
What do you like doing?
What's up?
What's your favorite sport?
You're pretty good.

UNIT 5

Gerunds
flying a kite
jogging
playing the guitar
playing tennis
reading a book
taking photographs

Adjectives
popular
unique

Expressions
He's hanging out.
Get a life.
He's such a bookworm!
Wait up.

UNIT 6

Nouns
acrobat
acrobatic
application
audition
clothes
clown
eyeglasses
juggling
performance
schedule
trampoline
T-shirt
video

Adjectives
big
high
long
loose
low
purple
short
small
tight

Verbs
fall
slip
wear

Expressions
How do I look?
I think it's too…
What do you think of this dress?
I'm not sure I like it.
How about these jeans?
They're great!
You look good in them.

UNIT 7

Nouns
Bermuda shorts
dance moves
miniskirt
necklace
opinion
pantsuit
pedal pusher
performance
stage

Verbs

Base form	Simple past form
call	called
clean	cleaned
finish	finished
hug	hugged
play	played
sneeze	sneezed
stay	stayed
study	studied
wash	washed
watch	watched

Past-time markers
a month ago
a week ago
last night
last year
yesterday
yesterday morning

Expressions
Congratulations!
I agree.
I don't agree.
That was nice of them.
What's your story?
You are awesome!
You just made my day.
You were great.
You're right.

UNIT 8

Nouns
horse
performer
recommendation
riding lessons
show
summer program

Verbs

Base form	Simple past tense of irregular verbs
be	was, were
break	broke
bring	brought
come	came
drive	drove
feel	felt
get	got
give	gave
go	went
grow	grew
has/have	had
hear	heard
hold	held
put	put
sleep	slept
stand	stood
take	took
teach	taught
tell	told
think	thought

Expressions
Can you believe that?
Don't be upset.
Hey, are you all right?
I can't wait.
I think he was unfair.
I'm upset about…

Useful Words and Expressions

UNIT 9

Nouns
lightning
storm
temperature
weather

Adjectives
afraid
cold
hot
nervous
scared
warm

Verbs
arrive
cry
imitate
shake
shiver
start

Expressions
What's the weather like today?
It's sunny.

UNIT 10

Nouns
continent
earthquake
elephant
garden
hippopotamus
monument
singer
statue
whale

Adjectives
bad
far
good
famous
funny
important
interesting
old
unfair

Expressions
Are you mad at me?
Should I be?
Which continent is smaller, Asia
　or Australia?
Which do you like better, hot dogs
　or hamburgers?
I like hamburgers better.

UNIT 11

Nouns
aspirin
cheekbones
doctor
entertainment
eyebrow
fax
musical
script

Adjectives
adventurous
artistic
careful
difficult
dramatic
emotional
reasonable
sensitive

Verb phrases
call the dentist *or* the doctor
get some rest *or* sleep
see a doctor *or* dentist
take an aspirin
take some cold medicine

Expressions
I don't feel well.
I feel silly.
I have a headache.
I think you should …
I'm sorry to hear that.
It's all right. I understand.
What should I do?
What's the matter?

UNIT 12

Verbs
Summer activities
attend summer camp
find a job
learn a new skill or hobby
take summer classes
train in athletics
travel/go abroad
volunteer

Expressions
What will you do this summer?
I might. . .
I'm not sure.
Come on, guys.
I want to apologize.